Anxiety: Finding the Better S… comforting truth with practi… entry topics. Every Christian counselor needs this resource for their clients.
—**Alice Churnock**, Licensed Professional Counselor

Liz has written a great resource that takes our spiritual life seriously and thoughtfully. . . . Liz is a caring and gifted communicator, and I will recommend this outstanding resource over and over again.
—**Jim Coffield**, Pastor; Psychologist; Former Professor,
Reformed Theological Seminary

An absolutely outstanding resource. . . . This book contains biblical richness and practical techniques to both relieve anxiety and give young people tools for coping for the rest of their lives.
—**Cameron Cole**, Founding Chairman, Rooted Ministries

Liz Edrington leads teens through practical meditations and thoughtful questions that remind and assure them that "God is our refuge and strength, an ever-present help in trouble" (Ps. 46:1). For teens who struggle with anxiety, this book is a gift!
—**Scott Coupland**, Professor of Counseling, Reformed Theological Seminary, Orlando

Writing with such honesty and warmth . . . Liz Edrington shows her anxious readers that the Jesus we meet in Scripture is not an abstract idea but a practical, reliable, and helpful Person.
—**Anna Meade Harris**, Senior Director of Content, Rooted Ministry

This book is timely, wise, Christ-honoring, and powerfully life-giving. . . . We all need this, not just teenagers. Let the conversations, the breathing (you'll get it once you read it!), and the healing begin.
—**Kelly M. Kapic**, Author, *You're Only Human*

Liz Edrington invites students to understand their anxiety—but even more to understand the faithfulness and goodness of their Father in heaven. Through this devotional, students really will discover themselves in God's story and will thus be grounded in the peace of God.

—**Mike McGarry**, Founder and Director, Youth Pastor Theologian; Author, *A Biblical Theology of Youth Ministry*

This thirty-one-day devotional engages the spectrum of what it means to be fully human. . . . Be ready for a fully human experience that will remind you of God's deep love for every ounce of your being.

—**Robert Row**, Student Ministries Director, seeJesus

In thirty-one daily doses of truth, beauty, and goodness from the story of God, Liz does the heavy lifting to help us to begin to write a new story. . . . I believe this book can provide encouragement for anyone who is ready to negate the power of anxiety in their life.

—**Tony Souder**, CEO, One Hundred Years; Founder, Pray for Me Campaign

I can't think of a more timely and needed resource for teenagers today than this! . . . This devotional is firmly rooted in God's Word; it is gracious and truthful and very practical. I plan to recommend it to youth leaders and parents alike!

—**Zach Wyatt**, Director, Youth Leader Collective

This is a book I didn't know I desperately needed. The freedom and grace that it offers are a massive gift to the church. It's so helpful, so practical, and so deeply Christ-centered: I wish every teenager could have a copy.

—**Kevin Yi**, College and Young Adults Pastor, Church Everyday, Northridge, California

ANXIETY

31-DAY DEVOTIONALS
FOR TEENAGERS

A P&R Publishing Series
in Partnership with Rooted Ministry

CHELSEA KINGSTON ERICKSON
Series Editor

ANXIETY

Finding the Better Story

LIZ EDRINGTON

P&R PUBLISHING

P.O. BOX 817 • PHILLIPSBURG • NEW JERSEY 08865-0817

For Marthy Ro, Becky Lanks, and Jenny Stew:
your wrestling encourages me,
your resilience inspires me,
and your friendship enlivens my soul.
God's faithfulness becomes clearer when I think of you.

Cover design by Jelena Mirkovic

Printed in the United States of America

Library of Congress Cataloging-in-Publication Data

Names: Edrington, Liz, author.
Title: Anxiety : finding the better story : 31-day devotionals for
   teenagers / Liz Edrington.
Description: Phillipsburg, New Jersey : P&R Publishing, [2023] | Summary:
   "Do you feel anxious? A lot? Learn more about what anxiety is-and about
   the hope, purpose, and comfort that the Bible gives you-in this 31-day
   devotional for teenagers"-- Provided by publisher.
Identifiers: LCCN 2022058466 | ISBN 9781629959139 (paperback) | ISBN
   9781629959160 (epub)
Subjects: LCSH: Anxiety--Biblical teaching. | Christian teenagers--Prayers
   and devotions. | Devotional calendars.
Classification: LCC BS680.A58 E37 2023 | DDC 242/.40835--dc23/eng/20230329
LC record available at https://lccn.loc.gov/2022058466

CONTENTS

CONNECTION ENJOYED

HOW TO UNDERSTAND ANXIETY

Stomach like a clenched fist. Palms sweating. Difficulty breathing. Merry-go-round mind spinning out of control.

These are classic symptoms of anxiety.

When I was in high school, I had to eat a meal at least three hours before my soccer games. Otherwise, a spaghetti dinner would haunt me throughout the entire game—and potentially make an ungraceful reappearance midfield.

My pregame anxiety was intense. And try as I might, I couldn't *talk* the nervousness away. I couldn't control it. It was powerful, annoying, and frustrating. I hated the way I had to organize my entire day around it.

As a teenager, I was just trying to survive my anxiety. Now, as a mental health counselor, I wonder what might have been different back then if I had better understood it. I've written this devotional so that, for the next thirty-one days, you might experience clarity and comfort in your stress and anxiety as you read about the hope God offers us through his Word.

From one anxious struggler to another: you are not alone. Let's dive in.

What Is Anxiety?

Most basically, anxiety is an emotion. It *isn't* part of our identity or personality. We can feel anxiety in our bodies when our hearts race, our breathing gets shallow, and our stomachs tense. Anxiety causes us to go on high alert whether we want to or not. Sometimes we pick at our skin, pull at our hair, or chew our nails. Anxiety often comes with worried thoughts and fear.

Anxiety may seem like an enemy, but it's actually our bodies' natural response to stress. Too much stress can be bad for us, but we all need good stress in order to grow. Think about how we learn to walk: our muscles have to go through stress to get stronger. We experience stress when we learn new skills on an instrument or in a sport or when we risk making new friends or having hard conversations. Anxiety may be uncomfortable, but it isn't *always* a bad thing.

When stressful things cause anxiety, the way we *respond* to that anxiety can make a huge difference in how overwhelming it becomes.

Here is an image I want you to remember: anxiety is like a big wave in the ocean that you have to ride out. Like anxiety, a wave is powerful. It is neither good nor bad. Yes, a wave can destroy sand castles—but it's also great for bodysurfing.

Imagine standing in front of a wave with your hand out in front of you and saying, "Stop, wave!" This would be completely ridiculous (although potentially entertaining), and we all know it wouldn't work. But this is how we often treat anxiety. We tell ourselves to just calm down already. In the end, our "Stop!" doesn't work; our anxiety bowls us over like an ocean wave would. We are defeated. Frustrated or embarrassed, we assume something must be wrong with us.

Having anxiety does not mean you don't have enough faith or are a "bad Christian." You are not *wrong* for having anxiety. Almost everyone feels anxious at some point or another. So if you can't stop the wave of emotion by force of will, how do you get through it?

Like waves, emotions rise and fall and take their course. They have a beginning, a middle, and an end. When you learn to ride out your emotions with God, to feel your way through them, they don't tend to knock you down quite as often. It may sound strange, but this may mean you need to *lean in* to your anxiety—as if you were bodysurfing that wave. Leaning in to your anxiety may be as simple as talking about it with someone you trust. Working through this devotional, whether alone or with a parent or youth leader, will go a long way toward this goal. Instead of wearing yourself out by yelling at the wave to stop, you're invited to look at God-given ways to live with your anxiety, to ride these emotions out from beginning to middle to end.

Sometimes the waves of anxiety just keep coming. Even then, this doesn't mean you've done anything wrong. It's a reminder that we're all works in progress. It's true for me too. I'm still not a professional anxiety bodysurfer, but I now have many stories of how Jesus has met me in beauty and power as I've struggled.

How Jesus Meets Us in Our Anxiety

The Lord is no less present with us when we are anxious and stressed out. In fact, he loves us *right in* our anxiety, and he offers us hope. He even gives meaning to our anxiety in light of his bigger story of redemption for humankind. To find that love, hope, and meaning, we look to the Word of God:

> I pray that out of his glorious riches he may strengthen you with power through his Spirit in your inner being, so that Christ may dwell in your hearts through faith. And I pray that you, being rooted and established [or grounded] in love, may have power, together with all the Lord's holy people, to grasp how wide and long and high and deep is the love of Christ, and to know this love that surpasses knowledge—that you may be filled to the measure of all the fullness of God. (Ephesians 3:16–19)

In the counseling world, we talk a lot about *grounding* when anxiety comes up. Tips, tricks, and techniques can be super helpful (and we will cover our fair share of these in this book). But ultimately we need to be grounded in something more powerful than ourselves. We need a trustworthy, grounding source of love and identity that isn't dependent on us—one that isn't dependent on our own knowledge, abilities, or emotions. Like Paul says in Ephesians, we need a love that is wider than our worst fears, longer than our what-ifs, higher than our greatest anxieties, and deeper than our pain. We need the love that surpasses knowledge, and we find it in the person of Jesus Christ.

In Jesus, we find comfort and hope for our struggle with anxiety. We find a God who can completely understand what it's like to experience stress, because he experienced it as a human himself. In fact, he was so overwhelmed at one point that he actually sweated blood (Luke 22:44). Jesus doesn't leave us on our own or impatiently tell us to "calm down." Instead, he draws near to us with deep compassion. He is the God-man who is *for* us and *with* us.

Not only can Jesus empathize with us, but he took it one step further. He sacrificed his life and was resurrected so that our story might be enfolded in his. In his story, death can never win. This means the lies and fears that haunt us in our anxiety won't win either. Our promised future is full of beauty and joy. As we walk with Jesus, he grounds us in his love. He is sinking our hearts, minds, and bodies deeper into his story of love: he died and rose so that we might come to know the freedom of living as his beloved people. In Christ, we are ultimately secure.

My prayer is that through this devotional you will come to find hope, purpose, and comfort for your anxiety in the person of Jesus. As you read the Scripture passages and practice prayerful breathing (see the Anxiety Toolkit), I pray you will find yourself more and more caught up in the big story of our triune God. He is one God in three persons: the Father, Jesus the Son, and the Holy Spirit. The story of his unstopping, unfailing, death-defeating, life-bringing love is *your* story. And the outcome is dependent on God's work and not your own—which means there is peace for you in this bigger story, even when you feel anxious.

Sometimes anxiety becomes so overwhelming that it interferes with normal life and may even cause panic attacks.

A panic attack is a surge of intense fear or terror that may be accompanied by a racing heart, shaking, nausea or dizziness, tightness in the chest, and scary thoughts like "I'm about to die."

If you are experiencing this extreme level of anxiety to the extent that your regular daily activities are interrupted, it is time to seek professional help from someone like a biblical counselor, a mental health counselor, a doctor, or a psychologist.

There is no shame in this—in fact, it is one of the most courageous steps you can take.

ANXIETY TOOLKIT

Jesus the Great Physician has given us some tools that can help us to move through our anxiety. As you read this devotional, return to this Anxiety Toolkit for practical grounding skills as you need them.

Tool #1: Grounded in Breath

It sounds too simple, but intentional breathing is one of the best tools for dealing with anxiety.

God designed our bodies to calm and settle themselves. When we first realize we are anxious, the very best thing we can do is take a deep breath and let it out slowly. Feel free to try it right now: breathe in through your nose while counting to four ("one, one thousand, two, one thousand," and so on), then breathe out through your mouth for four seconds. Try this a couple of times.

The same God with the power to create the world out of nothing breathed life into Adam's lungs in Genesis 2:7. He is the Creator and Sustainer of our lives, and he is closer to us than our breath as he walks with us.

Each entry of this devotional invites you to breathe in and breathe out while thinking of words that remind you of what you've just read. I recommend that you set your timer to at least sixty seconds to practice breathing with these truths in mind as you finish your time with Jesus.

Tool #2: Practicing Gratitude in the Now and Not Yet

The world is not all that it should be. Things are not perfect. Cars get into accidents. Friends betray us. We break promises. Our bodies don't work well all the time.

Right now, we live in a time that we call the *now and not yet*. This is the time period between when Jesus came to earth and when he will return. This is a waiting period. Jesus is *now* at work to bring hope and healing as king, and he has *not yet* come back to make everything right.

Jesus came to reconnect us to God	the now and not yet	Jesus returns to make everything right
↓	↓	↓
ca. 4 BC–AD 30	us right now	the future

Sin and Satan are still at work in the *now and not yet*. This is why, even if we are Christians, we still experience the discomfort of anxiety and wrestle with doubts. This is why death still exists. But God the Holy Spirit is with us in the *now and not yet*. He walks with us as we pray and wait for Jesus to return to make all things new. When Jesus comes back, sin and anxiety, death and doubt will be no more.

Gratitude is a very helpful practice in the *now and not yet*.

In our anxiety, it is good for us to look around and count the many ways God has seen us, loved us, and provided for us. It is okay if our gratitude lists don't fix or stop our anxiety. We make them in order to set our eyes on someone more powerful than our anxiety. Giving God thanks for specific blessings can help to distract us from intrusive thoughts and set our minds instead *on things above* (Colossians 3:2). We can be thankful for the clothes on our bodies, the sun in the sky, and the air we breathe, for our furry friends, our functioning feet, and our favorite foods. Be specific with the items on your list! Big or small, all gratitude is worth offering to God. He receives it with fondness and delight. Consider writing a list of ten things you are grateful for at the end of each devotional day.

Tool #3: Taste and See That the Lord Is Good

Psalm 34:8 tells us, "Taste and see that the LORD is good; blessed is the one who takes refuge in him."

In his wonderful creativity, the Lord gave us bodies that can reconnect us to the present moment when we feel disconnected. When we are overwhelmed by anxiety, we can use our five senses (sight, smell, touch, taste, and hearing) to experience God's goodness and take shelter in him.

The 5-4-3-2-1 exercise is a great way to do this. Look around and name five things you can see, four things you are touching, three things you can hear, two things you can smell, and one thing you can taste. It's okay if you need to imagine the things you can smell and taste.

Getting outside in nature is an ideal way to practice using your senses. It can also be helpful to slow way down and zoom in on the details of whatever you're noticing.

Science supports what Scripture tells us. God wired our bodies to help us to regulate our emotions and calm our minds. He made us for deep connection—to himself, one another, and ourselves. These exercises impact us biologically as we practice them. They bring healing by helping to reshape our patterns of thinking, feeling, and doing.

MADE FOR DEEP CONNECTION

"You have made us for yourself, O Lord, and our hearts are restless until they rest in you."
Augustine, **Confessions**

Anxiety makes us restless. It makes us desire all sorts of things. We want relief. We want comfort. We want hope, security, and love. We want to know if our lives have purpose and meaning.

In Scripture, we learn that God hardwired these desires into us. We have been designed for deep, secure, life-filled relationships with God, creation, ourselves, and one another. We also learn that all humans are image bearers of God, which means each one of us is valuable, lovable, and worthy of belonging.

When our anxiety whispers lies to us about our lives, we lean in to our relationship with our Creator, the one who crafted us lovingly in his image. We rest in the truths he tells us about our story.

Day 1

JESUS IS REST

Come to me, all who labor and are heavy laden, and I will give you rest. Take my yoke upon you, and learn from me, for I am gentle and lowly in heart, and you will find rest for your souls. (Matthew 11:28–29 ESV)

You will find rest for your souls.

It sounds too good to be true, doesn't it? If I were one of the worn-out people in the crowd at Capernaum listening to Jesus say these words, I would probably be thinking, "Bold statement, man. Who are you to say you can give rest for my soul?"

Good question! Jesus was the man who had drawn large crowds with his teaching and preaching. He had given sight to the blind, healed the sick, and performed many other miracles. And he was also the man who, outrageously, had just claimed to be God himself (Matthew 11:27).

As both God and man, Jesus knew exactly how anxious and burdened the people around him were, and he said, "Come to me." His heart went out to them, and he offered them what they needed for rest: himself.

Anxiety can be an incredible load. It weighs us down. Sometimes it is silent, pressuring us from the inside. Sometimes it nags like a pesky sibling who keeps tapping us on the shoulder. The more we ignore it, the more disruptive it gets. The meaner we are to it, the stronger it gets. Anxiety makes us feel heavy-laden.

Like the people at Capernaum, we are surrounded by many things that try to convince us we'll stop feeling heavy-laden if we *come to them*. Social media whispers, "If you get enough likes, you'll be worthy!" Political groups urge, "Join us, then you'll be on the right side of history!" Social mantras invite us: "Live your truth, and you'll be happy!" Consumerism entices us: "Buy this product, then you'll fit in!"

Some of these things may be helpful in the short run. They may provide a place for us to belong, a sense of cultural acceptance, and a hope that our lives will improve. But they lack the ultimate power and relief that the God who created the universe offers us when he says, "Come to me."

Here is what we find when we come to Jesus:

The peace of knowing that our anxiety will not defeat us; because in Christ, we know the end of our story, and it is one of beauty and joy (Revelation 21:1–5).

The assurance that our anxiety does not define us; because in Christ, our identity is that of sons and daughters of God (Romans 8:14–17; Galatians 4:6; Ephesians 1:5).

The promise that our anxiety is not pointless; because in Christ, God never wastes our struggles. He is at work redeeming painful and broken things (Romans 8:28).

The comfort of a God who meets us where we are; because in Christ, we aren't left on our own to figure things out. We are never alone; God is always with us (Matthew 1:23).

The *me* in "Come to me" makes all the difference in the world. Jesus himself is the only true rest for our anxious souls. He is so much more than a philosophy, a brand, an ideology, a self-help mantra, or a therapist. Jesus is love incarnate, God with skin on. He is gentle and lowly. He is kind and generous. He doesn't ask you to earn his love by performing well in school, by being the ideal son or daughter, or even by getting rid of your anxiety. He offers you his love with no strings attached. And he offers you something to *do* with even your worst anxiety: come to him.

Breathe in: **God is with me.**
Breathe out: **Jesus is rest for my heavy soul.**

We are invited to come to Jesus with all of ourselves—our thoughts, emotions, and bodies. What might it look like for you to draw near to God with your mind? With your emotions? With your body?

THE BIGGER STORY

In the beginning God created. . . . God made the wild animals according to their kinds, the livestock according to their kinds, and all the creatures that move along the ground according to their kinds. And God saw that it was good. (Genesis 1:1, 25)

Any time we hear "Once upon a time," we know we're about to hear a great story.

Similarly, "In the beginning" invites us into a story. But this is no fairy-tale introduction. Instead, we're welcomed into the true and beautiful story of God's love for his people and the world.

In this story, God is the author. He brings all things into being with creativity and intentionality. He doesn't haphazardly throw some plant, animal, and human ingredients into an earthly soup pot and stir it up, hoping for the best. He forms. He crafts. He creates with purpose and delight, and he calls his creation good.

King Jesus is at the center of this story, holding all things together (Colossians 1:17). When we put our trust in him, we become participants in his glorious plan to redeem all things. Our lives become defined by the grace and love of Jesus. We become a part of Christ's body—his family—and every hard, painful, and confusing chapter we experience becomes valuable in the wildly mysterious and beautiful story God is writing.

What sort of story is your anxiety telling you?

My anxiety is pretty nearsighted. It's a lot like the woman I saw at the bus stop yesterday. She'd clearly forgotten her glasses, so she was squinting about two inches from the map. She may have been able to see one small part of that map, but she couldn't see the whole thing. She was missing out on the bigger picture.

Anxiety tends to zoom in on specific worries without our even realizing it. When I write out the stories my anxiety is telling me or talk to a friend about them, I'm often surprised at what I discover. I hear fear after fear about my worth, my identity, my safety, and my future. And I hear only negative endings to each of my concerns.

"What if I introduce myself and they think I'm awkward?"

"What if I can't finish this assignment on time and fail?"

"What if my foot never heals and I can never run again?"

When our noses are pressed to the map as we try to figure our way out of our anxiety, we lose sight of the bigger story we're a part of. When we notice our stomachs tense, our minds spin, and our hearts race, it is time to return to the deeply good and beautiful story God is writing that began long before we were born.

This story is rooted in history, not mere philosophies or ideals. And in this story God has chosen you. He had a plan for your life before he even made the earth (Psalm 139:16), and he has promised to work all things toward his good (Romans 8:28).

When our anxiety shrinks the big story into smaller, fearful, more negative plotlines, we can look to Scripture to remember that we are a part of the more glorious story God is writing. In this story, our worth is secure. Our identity is secure. Our future is secure. In this story, our anxiety never has the final say over our lives, because God has the final say. He's already written the ending. Death will not win, and all will be made right (Revelation 21:3–4).

Breathe in: *God is a good author.*
Breathe out: *His story is my story.*

If you could see the thought bubbles of your anxiety, what would they be saying?

ORDER FROM CHAOS

*In the beginning God created. . . . And God
said, "Let there be . . ." (Genesis 1:1, 3)*

*In the beginning was the Word, and the Word was with
God, and the Word was God. He was with God in the
beginning. Through him all things were made. (John 1:1–3)*

Anxiety is a type of internal chaos.

When I'm anxious, I long for someone to bring peace to my body and mind—the way my seventh-grade teacher brought order to my class. She would cup her hands around her mouth and shout into the rowdy room: "And a hush fell over the crowd!" All the commotion and chatter would stop as we responded together, "Hushhhhhhhhh!"

There was great power in Ms. Doubet's words. They brought stillness and silence where there had once been chaos.

A similar dynamic is at work in the power of God's words— "Let there be"—in Genesis 1. The first thing they accomplish is to bring order from chaos. Genesis 1:2 describes the world as "formless and empty" at the beginning of time and says "darkness was over the surface of the deep." Without any shape or order yet, earth was like a swamp without borders.[1] When the writer of Genesis used the word *darkness*, he was referring to a chaotic place. Up wasn't up yet. Down wasn't down. It may not have been a class full of thirty chatting tweens, but things were wild.

God's words weren't just nice-sounding syllables that floated away on the wind. They tamed the dark confusion and formed all creation. They ordered day and night, land and sea. They gave shape to our world.

If I had tried to use Ms. Doubet's magic phrase in our class, my peers would have rolled their eyes and kept talking. I didn't have her authority and power. But as the author of our world,

God holds ultimate authority. His words can *bring life* to dead people, as when Jesus told Lazarus to "Come out!" (John 11:43). They can also *bring light* to blind eyes, as when he told the blind man to go and wash at the pool of Siloam (John 9:7). They can even *bring stillness*, as when he calmed the storm (Mark 4:39).

Jesus's words aren't just tips on how to live a happy life. His words actually *make* and *give* life itself. They provide structure where there is none. They also provide us with hope for our internal chaos as we struggle with anxiety. This is a huge part of why we read, listen to, and speak God's words (from Scripture) to one another.

When we just can't seem to turn down the volume of our anxiety, we can turn up the volume of God's words to us. We can listen to what he says *about* us: "Fear not, for I have redeemed you; I have called you by name, you are mine" (Isaiah 43:1 ESV). And we can listen to what he says *to* us: "Peace I leave with you; my peace I give you. I do not give to you as the world gives. Do not let your hearts be troubled and do not be afraid" (John 14:27).

God also gives power to *our* words. Naming, describing, and sharing our anxiety with someone we trust can help to tame it. Then we can offer it to the One who has the power to do far more than we can imagine. He is the One who gently loves and tends to us, offering himself as a "Hussssssssh" in the chaos as we learn to trust him with our anxiety even when it doesn't seem to change.

Breathe in: *The Word has the power to calm.*
Breathe out: *He loves me in the chaos.*

Spend some time putting words to your anxiety. Songs, poetry, and psalms can be helpful with this.

Day 4

GROUNDED IN CREATION

*Then the LORD God formed a man from the dust of the
ground and breathed into his nostrils the breath of life,
and the man became a living being. (Genesis 2:7)*

What comes to mind when you hear the word *mandrake*? If you're
like me, you conjure up an image of the shrieking creature from
Harry Potter and the Chamber of Secrets. A mandrake is a hideous
little beastie. It's a magical plant that looks like a cross between a
sweet potato and a baby. Its screeches can cause those who hear
it to become disoriented and confused and even to faint. It's
downright awful—not unlike the experience of being flooded by
anxiety.

When a mandrake is screaming, its greatest need is to be
planted in the ground. For a mandrake to go quiet, it needs its
little potato-y feet to be connected to the soil.

Thankfully, God created humans with more beauty than the
mandrake. But when we feel anxious, our need to be grounded is
pretty similar.

Genesis 2 tells us that humanity had an earthy beginning—
we were made from the dirt! God created us uniquely, as embodied souls. This means we aren't just bodies made to work. We
aren't just brains made to think. And we aren't just souls breathed
into being by God himself. We are a glorious combination of all
these ingredients. And it's important to consider that God didn't
place Adam—body and soul—in a library, a factory, or an arctic
tundra: he put him in a garden. Our whole self, like Adam's, was
designed to thrive in connection with the earth from which we
were formed.

Anxiety loves to *disconnect* us from reality. It draws our attention to potential disastrous scenarios. It distracts us with discomfort. It takes us out of the present moment and fixes us in a haze of

25

worry and confusion. Thankfully, God designed our bodies with built-in ways to calm and reconnect us when anxiety disconnects us. In the medical world, this is called the *mind-body connection*. We access this through our God-given senses.

Our bodies experience the world in both physical and emotional ways. God brilliantly gave us noses that smell, fingers that feel, eyeballs that see, tongues that taste, and ears that hear. When our minds hop on their hamster wheels of anxiety, we can draw our attention to one of our senses and engage with God's good creation.

When I feel anxious, I like to bring my attention to my feet on the ground (touch). I wiggle my toes and notice what the surface is like, whether I feel squishy socks, cold hardwood, or soft carpet. It's even better if I'm able to take a step outside in my bare feet. I'm not trying to fix or stop my anxiety; I'm just turning my attention to something else. In noticing the cool, prickly grass and the feel of my weight against the earth, I am drawn into the present moment with God. With every small detail I take in during this simple exercise, I notice my breath evening out, my stomach tension releasing, and my heartbeat slowing. Focusing on one of our senses has a biological way of quieting our anxiety and connecting us to the present moment.

Friend, when your anxiety disrupts and disconnects you, step outside and draw your full attention to your toes on the ground. Notice and describe the sensations you feel as you let your feet sink into the very dirt from which God lovingly created you. He loves to meet us through our senses as we enjoy his good creation.

Breathe in: *My body is a gift from God.*
Breathe out: *I can feel my toes on the ground.* (Actually practice feeling them!)

List three ways you could use your senses to enjoy God through his creation today.

MADE FOR CONNECTION WITH GOD AND ONE ANOTHER

*Then the LORD God said, "It is not good
that the man should be alone; I will make him
a helper fit for him." (Genesis 2:18 ESV)*

It is fascinating to think about Adam hanging out in creation before sin entered the world. He had the chance to take in all the beauty of the fruit trees, the flowers, and the creatures before brokenness ever flooded in. There was absolutely nothing wrong with the world at large, yet something about Adam's personal world was incomplete. There was no one to share the work and no one to enjoy the loveliness with him. The animals just wouldn't cut it. So God made a counterpart to man: he created woman. He gave Adam a friend, because it wasn't good for him to be alone.

One of the most beautiful parts of the Christian faith is the core truth that humans have been designed for relationships. We have been created for deep, secure connection with God and with one another. The need for friendships is written in our DNA. We've been made in the image of a God who is himself in eternal relationship: he is Father, Son, and Holy Spirit (Genesis 1:26). He constantly shares and offers love within the Trinity. Similarly, he knows us and invites us to know him and one another.

Have you ever had an experience of feeling truly understood in your anxiety? Like someone really *gets* the shape, feel, and craziness of your anxious mind?

When I'm really struggling, I've found that my default tends to be "You should know how to figure this out, Liz. You're a therapist." And I get busy trying to do just that. I try to fix it all on my own. I do the breathing. I practice gratitude. I use a grounding technique.

Yet nothing compares to inviting both God and a trusted, loving friend into my struggle.

"Hey Meg, do you have an hour for coffee on Friday? I need to talk it out. And I need prayer. My mind just won't stop racing."

When my friend really listens to me, loves me, and prays for me, something in me often shifts. She repeats back what I say to her and acknowledges how hard it is. I see care and compassion in her eyes. She empathizes with me, sharing with me how she has struggled too. And then she brings my anxiety before God in prayer, asking him to help.

In her presence and God's, I am known and loved in my powerlessness to fix my anxiety. Even if my anxiety hangs around, my perspective may change ("Oh hey, I am not alone in this!"). Or my hope for the future may change ("I don't have to bear this by myself"). I am reminded that I am *more* than my anxiety. I am a daughter of King Jesus. I am a beloved friend.

Today's words from Genesis remind us we aren't supposed to do this on our own. Humans weren't ever supposed to suffer alone, to celebrate alone, or to bear the discomfort of anxiety alone. We have been created to do life together—with God and with one another. We are made for relationships.

Loneliness can be fuel to the fire of anxiety ("No one knows how hard this is"). But we can courageously combat this by being vulnerable and sharing with a friend and with God. We can live into the reality at the heart of Christianity: we were made to be known and loved. God desires to be in relationship with us, and he longs for us to experience relationship with him.

Breathe in: *I am not alone in my anxiety.*
Breathe out: *I am known, and I am loved.*

If God were sitting across from you right now, what would you share with him about your life? Who is a friend you might consider sharing that with?

HOW WE BECAME DISCONNECTED

*So when the woman saw that the tree was good for food, and
that it was a delight to the eyes, and that the tree was to be
desired to make one wise, she took of its fruit and ate, and
she also gave some to her husband who was with her, and
he ate. Then the eyes of both were opened, and they knew
that they were naked. And they sewed fig leaves together
and made themselves loincloths. (Genesis 3:6–7 ESV)*

Can you remember the first time you realized something wasn't
quite right with the world? Maybe it was the first time you fell
and skinned your knee as a toddler. Or maybe it was when that
pigtailed bully in preschool stole your purple plastic hair dryer
(maybe that was just me).

At some point, we all have to deal with the question "What is
wrong with this world?" It is natural to want to know why things
don't seem to be the way they are supposed to be. Wars break out.
Parents get divorced. Little kids lie. Tsunamis wipe out whole
villages. Cancer exists. Something is off: the world seems broken.

We learn in Genesis 1 and 2 that God desires a relationship with his people. He wants to be in deep, loving connection
with his image bearers. He cares for them, and he wants them
to thrive. He even gave the first couple instructions for how to
thrive, telling them to fill the earth, tame it, and rule over the animals (Genesis 1:28). He also invited them to eat the fruit from all
the trees of the garden except for one (Genesis 2:16–17).

God wants his people to trust him. He wants what is best for
them, for us.

Instead, Adam and Eve decided to do life their own way, and
all human beings since have followed after them. They believed
that they knew better than God what was best for them. So they
took the fruit from the forbidden tree and ate.

With this decision to disobey God, sin flooded into the world. Like a drop of dye spreading out in a cup of water, all aspects of the world became tainted by sin. Creation was affected, which is why we see tornadoes and hurricanes, floods and forest fires. And every part of humanity was and is affected, including our minds, bodies, emotions, wills, and motivations. This means we don't think perfectly, we don't feel perfectly, our bodies aren't perfect, and we don't have perfect willpower or motives. The taint of sin disconnects us from God, one another, and even ourselves. You aren't crazy: the world is not as it should be.

We weren't made to live in the fear and shame that Adam and Eve experienced after they first sinned. We weren't made to hide from God or to worry about what others think of us. We were made to live face-to-face with God in paradise. We were made to be in loving, perfect relationship with him and one another.

The whole Bible is a story of God's never-stopping, loving pursuit of his people. His heart is for all to be made right. He longs to see us reconnected to himself. He longs for the whole world to be restored to the goodness he originally intended. As you'll read about in the following days, this is why Jesus came: to provide the ultimate reconnection to God. In Jesus, we have hope for our anxiety. In Jesus, we can be honest when things don't seem right. Although sin will be a part of our world until he returns, Jesus is at work *right now* making all things right. He is in control, and his plan is unfolding perfectly, even amidst the brokenness we see.

Breathe in: *I am not crazy. All is not right.*
Breathe out: *God is making things right.*

What is something you want to be honest with God about, knowing there is nothing you could possibly do to make him love you any less?

30

GOD'S DESIRE FOR RECONNECTION

*Then the eyes of both of them were opened, and they realized they
were naked; so they sewed fig leaves together and made coverings
for themselves. Then the man and his wife heard the sound of the
Lord God as he was walking in the garden in the cool of the day,
and they hid from the Lord God among the trees of the garden. But
the Lord God called to the man, "Where are you?" (Genesis 3:7–9)*

Have you ever wondered why God asked, "Where are you?" in the
garden? He's the Creator of the universe! He knows everything.
So what's the deal with this question?

One of the great themes we see throughout the Bible is God's
loving pursuit of his people. Over and over again, his people run
away from him and hide. And over and over, he invites them
back. He is unlike any other god. He doesn't require us to get our
acts together before he comes for us. He comes for us just as we
are. And he never stops pursuing, no matter how far we run, no
matter how well we hide.

In today's Scripture, Adam and Eve had just disobeyed God
and chosen their own path over his. Sin had flowed into them,
bringing fear, shame, and disconnection. As a result, they hid
when they heard the sound of God in the garden.

Adam and Eve hid from God in two ways. They crouched
behind some trees. They also covered their naked bodies with fig
leaves. I can imagine them thinking, "Please don't look at me.
Look at all this leafy green camouflage instead."

Shame and anxiety often make me want to hide too. I don't
want anyone to see how much I'm struggling. So I get to managing my own garden camo. In high school, I hid behind academic
performance, athletic accomplishments, and Christian activities.
I put on a good face, covering my struggle with the fig leaves
of people-pleasing, perfectionism, and positivity—anything to

distract others from my anxious heart. It was easier to show my niceness and my hard work than to let others see what was really going on beneath the surface.

But God sees our hearts even when we are afraid to see them ourselves. And he moves toward us. His gentle, engaging question to Adam and Eve ("Where are you?") is not a question of unknowing. It is purely an invitation to connect. It shows us that no matter how many fig leaves we wrap ourselves in, no matter how many trees we hide behind, God is never put off. Instead of being distracted, annoyed, or disappointed by his hiding humans, he graciously invites them to come back to him, where love and forgiveness await. He warmly and patiently pursues them.

Even if we get confused about where our garden camo ends and *we* begin ("Am I really a positive person, or am I being positive to hide my anxiety?"), God's love pursues us deep into the vortex of our anxiety, and deeper yet into the shame that often fuels it. His love always invites us to come back into relationship with him. His desire for reconnection with us cannot be thwarted by our best attempts to hide.

God's seemingly simple question in the garden is a hopeful glimpse of the total reconnection to him that we're offered through Jesus's incarnation, death, and resurrection. It is an expression of his never-failing, always-pursing love, which will never give up on you.

Breathe in: *Even when I hide*—
Breathe out: *God will never stop pursuing.*

What is some of the garden camo you use to hide from others?

32

CONNECTION SECURED

For I am convinced that neither death nor life, neither angels nor demons, neither the present nor the future, nor any powers, neither height nor depth, nor anything else in all creation, will be able to separate us from the love of God that is in Christ Jesus our Lord. (Romans 8:38–39)

Although it can feel like our anxiety separates us from all that is good or hopeful, we are reminded that nothing can separate us from the love of God. We are secure in the finished work of Christ, meaning the what-ifs of anxiety turn into even-ifs.

Even if the person in front of you thinks you're ridiculous, you are secure in Christ's love.

Even if you fail this paper, exam, or assignment, you are secure in Christ's love.

Even if you don't make the team, cast, or ensemble, you are secure in Christ's love.

Even if your parents' marriage ends, you are secure in Christ's love.

Even if you can't help your brother, sister, or friend with their depression, you are secure in Christ's love.

Even if you don't get into the college you want to, you are secure in Christ's love.

Even if you feel stained and unlovable, you are secure in Christ's love.

Even if you don't get many likes or followers, you are secure in Christ's love.

Even if you are awkward, you are secure in Christ's love.

Even if the person you hope will like you ignores you, you are secure in Christ's love.

ANCHORED IN GOD'S PROMISES

Because God wanted to make the unchanging nature of his purpose very clear to the heirs of what was promised, he confirmed it with an oath.... We have this hope as an anchor for the soul, firm and secure. It enters the inner sanctuary behind the curtain, where our forerunner, Jesus, has entered on our behalf. (Hebrews 6:17, 19–20)

In high school, hope seemed like a lofty thing to me. I imagined it as something light and floating. I *hoped* I would make a good grade on an exam. I *hoped* I would get into a good college. I *hoped* I'd get asked on a date. I *hoped* my parents' marriage would get better.

Anxiety often crept up on this hope like a bully, taunting, "But what if you don't get what you want? What if it doesn't all work out?" My brain would toss and turn, asking worried what-ifs.

When I get caught up in the what-ifs, I need the anchoring hope Hebrews talks about to ground my heart, mind, and body. I need God to sink my whole being into the greater reality of his unchanging purpose.

From all eternity, God's purpose has been to fill the world with his glory and love. One specific way he does this is by making a family for himself. We see this through the covenant promise (oath) he made with Abraham (Genesis 12:1–3). Even though Abraham was super old and it seemed impossible, God promised to bless him with many descendants. In the New Testament, we find that the promise to Abraham was ultimately fulfilled in Jesus's death, making all who trust in him children of Abraham (Galatians 3:7).

When you and your friend hold up your pinkies and link them to swear that you'll keep your end of the bargain, your promise is dependent on each of you being faithful to that promise. You both have to follow through. But with God's promise to Abraham, he actually swore the oath *on himself*—the only one who is perfectly trustworthy and true. He is literally incapable of lying or breaking his promises. When Christ died, it was like God was holding his own pinkie—doing what he promised so long ago. In the same way, he has upheld your half of the bargain, paying the penalty for your sin.

There is something distinctly beautiful about the way our Christian hope is based on God's faithfulness and not our own.

This means the hope of God cannot fail you. It isn't optimism or a silver lining. It isn't a short-lived positive feeling. It is a rock-solid reality found in God's faithfulness to his promises throughout history. (This is why we study the Bible!) God has proven himself trustworthy over and over. And the epitome of this unshakable hope is found in the person of Jesus. His resurrection assures us that all God's promises for us are true.

No matter how much our minds and hearts sway like a ship at sea. No matter how many times we get caught up in our anxiety. We are anchored to the hope we have in Jesus.

This hope runs deeper than our anxiety. It is a hope that outweighs our worst worries. It isn't based on knowing the answers to our what-ifs. It isn't even dependent on our ability to *be hopeful*.

This hope is secured by the One who keeps all God's promises. He is incapable of failing us. He is incapable of letting us go. When we struggle to believe it, when we can't even feel it, our anchor—Jesus—holds us fast. His unshakable love cannot be uprooted.

Breathe in: *Even in my worries*—
Breathe out: *I am anchored in the love of Christ.*

What is a promise of God you want to anchor yourself in today?

SECURE IN GOD'S GRACE

You see, at just the right time, when we were still powerless,
Christ died for the ungodly. Very rarely will anyone die for a
righteous person, though for a good person someone
might possibly dare to die. But God demonstrates
his own love for us in this: While we were still
sinners, Christ died for us. (Romans 5:6–8)

What is love, anyway?

We say things like "I love tacos" and "I love basketball" and also "I love you." We watch shows where people fall in and out of love. We're told to follow our hearts. Yet sometimes our hearts aren't reliable in the love arena. Sometimes they don't fill with the weighty affection they once held for a boyfriend or girlfriend. And parents? Sometimes we struggle not to roll our eyes in disrespect.

In the Romans passage today, we read about the truest and realest love available: we read about Jesus. His love is the yardstick by which we measure all other loves. As 1 John 3:16 tells us, "This is how we know what love is: Jesus Christ laid down his life for us." Jesus *is* love with skin on. He is the most perfect picture of love that's ever existed.

So what is the nature of his love? Does it depend on how good we are? Does it depend on how much we pray? Does it depend on how well we care for those around us?

The good news of the gospel is this: while we were *yet* sinners, Christ died for us. This love depends *on him*. Before we trusted him, he died for us. Before we even knew we needed him, he died for us. While we still chose to make ourselves the kings and queens of our own lives (instead of making him the King of our lives), he died for us. He loved us *first*, and he loved us unconditionally. This is the grace of God.

Grace makes no earthly sense. It is undeserved. It is unearned. It is a gift offered to us *totally* based on the character of God and not our own character. It is based on his actions, not ours. It meets us in Christ when we have nothing to offer—when we feel unlovable and unworthy. It hunts us down when we feel out of control—when we feel we have no power to change. It pursues us even as we reject it.

When we read that Jesus sacrificed his life on the cross *for us*, we are reading about a love that was willing to give up *everything* for our sake. That is how much God wanted to be in relationship with us. That is how much he wanted us to know our belovedness. He was willing to face death for us. There is no place he is not willing to go for us.

Reread the above verses from Romans 5. We are loved *in* our anxiety. We are not loved *in spite of* our anxiety. Jesus doesn't roll his eyes at our struggle or sigh because of our inability to get over it. He doesn't overlook it or ignore it. He sees every part of our glorious and broken selves, and he draws near to us. His grace cannot be thwarted by our fear, our worry, or our stress. His grace meets us just as we are.

When we're rocked by the twists and turns life throws us, we can remember we are secured in God's love by the grace of Jesus. This love will never stop pursuing us. This grace is limitless. Christ demonstrated his love for us in this: while we were still rebelling against him, he died for us. This is the Love who will never let go of us.

Breathe in: *Even in my insecurity—*
Breathe out: *God's love pursues me.*

When have you seen or heard of undeserved love being given to someone? Your example could be from a book, a show, a movie, or real life.

Day 10

POWER IN GOD'S WORD OVER US

When he had received the drink, Jesus said, "It is finished."
With that, he bowed his head and gave up his spirit.
(John 19:30)

When we face hard things like making a decision about college or figuring out what to do about an unhealthy relationship, people often try to encourage us with words like "You do you" or "Do what makes you happy." When we struggle to believe we are worthy of being liked or belonging, they say, "Just believe you are worthy" or "Act like you belong."

These recommendations sound promising, don't they? It seems like they might really help.

But what is the belief at the core of all this advice?

That it's all up to you.

It's up to you to "do you" rightly. It's up to you to make yourself happy. It's up to you to believe you're worthy enough. It's up to you to try endlessly to think, feel, believe, or do something *enough*. And if it isn't working, well, try harder.

But what if there is something more for us? What if there is a far greater power offered to us by Someone outside us? Someone with more authority than an influencer, a bully, a principal, a parent, or a president. Someone with authority over death.

Jesus's statement on the cross "It is finished" is far more powerful than any self-help mantra. It is the Word of God spoken over his people, announcing, "Your debt (of sin) has been paid. You are free." It is the assurance by the all-powerful King of the universe that we no longer have *anything* to earn, prove, or fear. His death on the cross is the sacrifice that changes everything.

Christ's death declares forgiveness for each one of our failures. It declares freedom from any lie that tells us we must gain our worth or make ourselves *enough*.

When we hear a nagging word of accusation in our heads that just won't go away ("You should have done this" or "You shouldn't have done that") . . . in Christ, *it is finished*.

When we can't stop the freight train of worry about the future from barreling down on us ("What if I fail?" "What if they reject me?" "What if they think I'm stupid?" "What if I fall apart?") . . . in Christ, *it is finished*.

This means we can turn all our striving for worthiness, our striving for success, and our striving for belonging over to Jesus. His death secures our identity as beloved children of God. His word over us has the same power that brought all creation into being (John 1:1–3). And his word over us is final. Our struggle to believe this truth and to trust God's goodness doesn't have a drop of the power that God's word has over us.

The power offered to us in Christ is one that has defeated sin, Satan, and death. And it is at work *in us* through the Holy Spirit. Satan often whispers lies about who we are and what our future will be. But God's reminder to us is this: *It is finished. You are mine. Anxiety can never have the final say over your life because I have the final say. My final say is love: "See what great love the Father has lavished on us, that we should be called children of God! And that is what we are!" (1 John 3:1). My final say is hope: that an everlasting life of joy awaits you in the new heavens and new earth (Revelation 21:1–5).*

Breathe in: *When I'm tempted to believe anxiety's word over me—*
Breathe out: *It is finished.*

What area of earning, proving, or fear in your life needs the words "It is finished" spoken over it today?

Day 11

HOPE IN GOD'S VICTORY

The angel said to the women, "Do not be afraid,
for I know that you are looking for Jesus, who
was crucified. He is not here; he has risen, just as
he said. Come and see the place where he lay."
(Matthew 28:5–6)

Singing in front of people is terrifying for me. Just imagining it, I feel my breath shorten, my jaw tightens, and heat rises in my throat. I am swallowed up by discomfort.

My therapist, Monica, helped me work through this. We talked the day before I was to lead worship for chapel in seminary. She asked, "What is the worst that could happen when you get up there?" Then she encouraged me to play that (imagined) movie out to the very last scene.

I paused and asked myself, "What are you *most* afraid of, Liz?"

I realized I was afraid I'd mess up and embarrass myself. And if I did that, people would think I was ridiculous for trying to lead worship. And if they thought I was ridiculous, maybe they wouldn't like me. And if they didn't like me, maybe that meant I was unlovable.

Step by step, I took the story my anxiety was telling me to the very last scene. There, I discovered a powerful lie that was fueling my fear: *I am unlovable.*

Today's passage shines light into our darkest scenes. Our fears would have us believe they will get the last word. But the resurrection of Jesus proves otherwise.

The women in Matthew 28 were disciples of Jesus, his close friends. Seeing him crucified three days earlier had been devastating—the Son of God was not supposed to *die*. Their worst fear had been realized. So they went together to his tomb to grieve.

Imagine their shock and wonder when the earth shook and

an angel began speaking to them (Matthew 28:2–3). In seconds, their fear-come-true was reversed. The Lord was alive!

If Jesus didn't rise from the dead, Christianity doesn't offer any real hope. But the death of Jesus is not the end of his story or ours. Because Jesus defeated death, the end of our story is a new heavens and new earth. In our future is a joyful feast in the presence of God. There will be no tears, grief, or pain (Revelation 21:4). We will live free of anxiety with renewed bodies that allow us to enjoy God's goodness to the full.

Funny story: I *did* mess up leading worship that next day. I began in the wrong key and had to interrupt a whole crowd of people to start over. Instead of being mortified, I chuckled. The worst had happened, and the lies of my terror hadn't won out. I'd faced them already. I knew my better ending.

"He is not here; he has risen" means that the most powerful lies hiding beneath all of our fears cannot ultimately win. Jesus's defeat of death secures the good and true ending of our story. This means we can *lean in* to the lies our fear is telling us. We can move *through* them, knowing they do not have the last word.

The resurrection of Jesus means hope for our greatest imagined catastrophes. Even if they happen, our future is secure. Death, and all of our worst fears realized, cannot win in the end.

Breathe in: *Even if the worst happens—*
Breathe out: *Death cannot win.*

Consider something that scares you, and play the movie to the very last scene. What lie might be fueling your fear? How can the resurrection bring hope into that fear?

A HELPER WHEN WE STRUGGLE

But the Helper, the Holy Spirit, . . . he will teach you all things and bring to your remembrance all that I have said to you. Peace I leave with you; my peace I give to you. Not as the world gives do I give to you. Let not your hearts be troubled, neither let them be afraid. (John 14:26–27 ESV)

Friend, take a deep breath. Feel the air move into your nose and down into your lungs. Feel your ribcage expand. Consider how the oxygen you've just taken in glides to its final destination in your bloodstream. At some point in the journey, it is absorbed into your body. In a way, the O2 becomes closer to you than your very skin.

It is hard to imagine that the Holy Spirit is even closer to us than this. When we put our trust in Jesus, we are united to God completely. We become a house for the Holy Spirit (1 Corinthians 6:19). We are forever made into a new creation—*and the Holy Spirit is with us at all times, closer than the air we breathe.* We are never again left to do life on our own.

In today's passage, Jesus talks about leaving us the Helper—the third person of the Trinity—to continue to teach us and to help us to remember what he has said. Jesus knows we need help remembering who we are, who God is, and the reality of God's bigger story at work. He also knows we'll need calming. We'll need assurance. We'll need peace.

This means Jesus isn't surprised when we struggle. He isn't angry or disappointed. Even when we are frustrated with ourselves for being anxious, when our minds get stuck spiraling in worries, Jesus isn't caught off guard. He is ever ready to offer us kindness.

It reminds me of when my sweet golden retriever hears thunder. Bella's ears flatten, and her whole backside curls under her body. She scurries to me quickly with desperate, upturned eyes. She has no idea what's going on. She just knows she's terrified.

I often say to Bella something similar to what Jesus says in this passage: "Don't be afraid, li'l dowg. Don't worry. I'm here with you, and it's going to be okay." My tone is gentle and compassionate. My heart for her is peace. I'm not telling her to actually stop feeling anxious (as if she could control that). Instead, I'm inviting her to come to me for comfort.

Think of how people have tried to "help" you with your anxiety. Sometimes we get advice that doesn't bring relief in the long run. Or we hear incredibly unhelpful words like "Calm down, you're being irrational" or "Think of how much worse it could be" or "You're making a big deal out of nothing." But the Helper leaves us with something unlike anything the world offers.

In the Holy Spirit, we aren't left with advice. We are given the very presence of God. He offers us peace that is more than a feeling of relief or calm; it is the assurance that we are kept safe and held firm in the good story God is writing. He is always there to help us—*especially* when we can't help ourselves.

Take a deep breath. The Helper is closer to you than the air flowing through your body at this very moment. Even your *longing* for him to help is a sign that he is at work. He ties you to a future where your worries are no more. He reminds you of times he's brought you through your fear in the past. He is with you now as you ask for him to breathe his peace into every limb and every corner of your mind.

Breathe in: *Even when I don't feel peaceful—*
Breathe out: *I am held and kept safe by the Helper.*

Often we respond impatiently, fearfully, or angrily to our anxiety. Write out a response to your anxiety that reflects the gentle, compassionate way Jesus responds to people.

Day 13

GOD DRAWS NEAR WHEN WE FEAR

*And in the fourth watch of the night [Jesus] came to them,
walking on the sea. But when the disciples saw him walking on
the sea, they were terrified, and said, "It is a ghost!" and they
cried out in fear. But immediately Jesus spoke to them, saying,
"Take heart; it is I. Do not be afraid." (Matthew 14:25–27 ESV)*

The way Jesus handled his disciples' fear is so different from the way we handle our own.

Jesus is gentle and compassionate. He is tenderly comforting. He reassured his disciples by identifying himself to them. They knew the sound of his voice and would have felt relieved as he began speaking to them. "Do not be afraid" was an invitation to relax, not a shaming reprimand.

How different would this story be if Jesus had yelled at the disciples for feeling afraid? What if he had hollered at them, "You fools. You shouldn't feel anxious. You should know I can do anything!"

Jesus does *not* do this here (nor anywhere in Scripture). But how often do we do this to ourselves?

If anxiety had a shadow, it would be shame—the *shoulds* and *shouldn'ts* that often follow anxiety wherever it goes.

"I *should* be grateful, not anxious. I'm glad I was invited to my friend's house."

"I *should* stop worrying and calm down. It's going to be fine."

"I *shouldn't* be so stressed. This isn't a big deal."

It is amazing how often we tell ourselves what we *should* or *shouldn't* feel, as if we could directly *control* what we experience emotionally. In fact, many of us feel ashamed for feeling anxious (in our heads, we might hear, "I feel stupid for feeling . . ." or "I feel bad for feeling . . ."). In reality, shame only makes things worse.

When we shame ourselves over our emotions (the *shoulds* and *shouldn'ts*), they don't just go away. Their energy stores up in our bodies in different ways. This is why I had horrible stomach pain and nausea when I was working sixty hours a week. And it's sometimes why we have headaches or other types of pain in our bodies. Anxiety can be a sign we have a lot of emotion stored up in our bodies. Our emotion is made to be seen, felt, and shared with others who can bear our burdens with us. We see this with Jesus, who invites his friends to entrust their fear to him and let him bear that burden with them.

Have you ever held in a sneeze? It's painful. It needs to make its way out. It's ridiculous to imagine telling yourself, "You shouldn't sneeze. You're stupid for feeling like you want to sneeze." Sneezes and emotions both need to be released.

But we know there's a time and a place for them as well. We don't want to sneeze on the person sitting in front of us in school. We want to make sure our sneeze has a safe place to land. It would be far better to identify that we need to sneeze, choose the right place to aim our noses, and then sneeze away. The same is true with our emotions, although how we express them may look or sound different depending on our culture or family background.

The first and best place to aim our emotions is Jesus, the one who gently tells us, "Take heart; it is I." He is the one who already sees and knows us and loves us to the very depths of our emotions. The Ruler of heaven and earth invites us to share with him, to let him be our friend. He invites us to hear his powerful voice—the one that calms our storms as he says, "Do not be afraid." For he is with us, and he never leaves us on our own.

Breathe in: *Even when I fear—*
Breathe out: *I can take heart in the One who is with me.*

What are your common "I shouldn't feel _____"s or "I should feel _____"s?

Day 14

NEVER REJECTED BY GOD

All those the Father gives me will come to me, and whoever comes to me I will never drive away. (John 6:37)

If you've ever worried about what someone else might be thinking of you, you're not alone. How much of our lives do we spend fearing others' opinions of us? Fearing their judgment?

"They're going to think I'm awkward." "I'm going to look so stupid." "If they knew ____ about me, they'd totally reject me."

One of the things we know from Genesis 1 and 2 is that we've been designed for relationships. We're made for deep friendship with God and with one another. We long to be accepted. Ultimately, we find belonging by being brought into God's family, the body of Christ. We are welcomed because of Jesus's finished work on the cross—not anything we've done. We don't have to earn our worthiness; Jesus has done that.

In everyday interactions, it sure seems like we have to prove ourselves, doesn't it? We worry we need to be cool enough, smart enough, athletic enough, beautiful enough. We have to know the current lingo and see the most recent trending content. Otherwise we're irrelevant. We don't fit in. We might be rejected.

Today's verse explains that we are accepted completely by God through Jesus. We are held secure in God's family by none other than the Creator himself. He will never turn his back on us. When Jesus took our sin to the cross, the Father temporarily rejected his own Son. This punishment for sin meant that he would never have to reject us. Through Christ's sacrifice, God's love says, "You're *always* wanted and welcome. Nothing you do (or don't do) can cause me to reject you." His love meets us with kindness when we are rejected by a friend, peer, or family member. His love gives us courage to move through our worries about what others might think of us.

If you worry that your struggle with a secret addiction may lead to rejection by your family, God accepts you in Christ.

If you worry that confusion over your sexuality may lead to rejection by your friends, God accepts you in Christ.

If you worry that you're too awkward to ever belong to the group you want to be a part of, God accepts you in Christ.

If you worry that you're too sinful for God to love you, or you're not "sinful enough" for him to care about you, God accepts you in Christ.

Jesus's welcoming love extends to every anxious atom in your body—to every worried, numbed, or frustrated part of you. He will never drive you away (John 6:37).

Imagine what that might be like. It makes me think of the Alcoholics Anonymous group I visited once for an assignment in grad school. Some folks wore stained clothes. Some were in suits. Some smelled of body odor, others of cologne. Some smiled, and some made no eye contact. Yet every single person was greeted warmly in the same way I was: "Welcome, Liz. We're glad you're here. Keep coming back."

This is a picture of the loving acceptance Jesus offers to every part of us—especially those parts we worry about. He invites us into his grace where these parts can find hope, purpose, and healing—if not now, then most certainly on the last day when they are fully redeemed. All will be made right.

Breathe in: *When I worry I will be rejected—*
Breathe out: *God accepts me fully in Christ.*

Which part of you do you most worry about being rejected? Write about what it would be like to imagine that part being valued and welcomed just as I was welcomed.

IDENTITY SECURED

Without knowledge of self there is no knowledge of God.
Without knowledge of God there is no knowledge of self.
John Calvin, The Institutes of the Christian Religion

I am a daughter, a sister, a friend, a professor, and a counselor. I have been a soccer player, a coach, an EMT, a youth minister, and a McDonald's employee. I have red hair, freckles, and a club foot deformity. I'm attracted to men. Are these things my identity? Am I defined by them?

"Who are you?" is a complex question to answer, isn't it?

Does our experience of our sexuality determine our identity? Does the team, group, or subculture we belong to give us our identity? Is our identity based on some feature we have or on our family? What happens when these things change—do we lose our identity?

More and more, we hear messages about "living our truth." They tell us our truth is up to us to figure out and define. That our truth will give us our identity and that we then have to maintain it. I think of influencers who gain popularity by representing a cause or entertaining us in some way. They have to spend a lot of time maintaining their platform, cultivating their identity. Their worth is validated by likes or followers. But is that lasting?

In Christianity, we have a fixed point. We have an unchanging God who calls himself "I AM" (Exodus 3:14). And our worth is secure because we are his image bearers. Furthermore, ultimate truth is revealed in the person of Jesus who calls himself "the way and the truth and the life" (John 14:6). It's not that all truths lead to him; he *is* the way, the truth, and the life. We get to receive truth and identity from him. We don't earn, create, prove, or maintain our identity: it is given to us in Christ.

In this section, we will explore what it means to have our identity secured in Christ. Knowing who we are is intricately tied up with knowing who he is. We will be many things in our lives, but the surest, steadiest, most primary and anchoring is this: we are *his*.

Day 15

BELOVED SONS AND DAUGHTERS

And when Jesus was baptized, immediately he went up from the water, and behold, the heavens were opened to him, and he saw the Spirit of God descending like a dove and coming to rest on him; and behold, a voice from heaven said, "This is my beloved Son, with whom I am well pleased." (Matthew 3:16–17 ESV)

In high school, I felt a lot of pressure to find my identity. If I studied hard enough, maybe I'd get into a college and become a UVA Cavalier or a UNC Ram. If I played well enough in my sports, maybe I'd make it into my high school's hall of fame. I wasn't artsy enough for the theater or photography groups. I wasn't confident enough for the popular group. I remember wondering, "How will I know when I've *found* my identity?"

We live in a time when we hear conflicting things about our identity. We're told that who we're attracted to and how we experience our gender is who we are. We're also told, "No one can tell you who you are. It's up to you to decide." Various groups offer us belonging if we subscribe to their ideologies: "If you think and act like us, *you're in.*" But that also means "If you change, or if you disagree with something, you're out." The world says it's up to us to earn, create, and maintain our identity.

That's a lot of pressure. For me, that expectation is stressful, exhausting, and anxiety-inducing.

If our sexual attractions change, do our identities change? If we say the wrong things, will our groups kick us out? If we get injured and can't perform academically or athletically, what then?

In the Christian story, our identity is *given* to us. It isn't based on our achievements or failures. It isn't based on our sexuality. It isn't based on our likes or dislikes. It isn't based on our abilities or our friend group. It isn't based on our personality or popularity. It's based on two unshakable realities: the unchanging character of our triune God and the finished work of Jesus on the cross. Through this, God invites us to be *his beloved children*. With him, we don't achieve our identity; we receive it.

In today's verses, we read about the Father extending his love to the Son through the Holy Spirit. We see the Trinity at work, and we hear the *powerful* words that identify our Savior. Those same words remind us of our own spiritual adoption. Through Christ's perfect life on our behalf, we become unstoppably loved sons and daughters of God.

God does not love you abstractly. He loves you *particularly* and *specifically*. He chose *you* to belong to his family. He knows your name (Isaiah 43:1; John 10:3) and the number of hairs on your head (Luke 12:7). He is a good Father who will stop at nothing to make you know the depths of his love for you. He not only loves you but *likes* you. He delights in you (Zephaniah 3:17). He has *made you his*, which means you are left to discover, daily, what it means to be his child. You have nothing to earn, nothing to prove. His love requires no maintenance. Your identity as *beloved* has been set on you by the One who knows you better than you know yourself.

The groups you belong to will likely change over time. But your identity as a beloved son or daughter of God can never change. His words over us, through Christ, remain the same. "This is my beloved son or daughter. I chose this one. This one is mine" (see Isaiah 43:1; Ephesians 1:4–5). In Jesus, our identity is secure.

Breathe in: *I am a beloved son or daughter.*
Breathe out: *My belonging is sealed by the Holy Spirit.*

Think of a place of stress, fear, pain, or anxiety in your life. This is the very place God's love is set on you, where your identity as **beloved** has been locked in. Use the breathing prayer above to imagine what it would be like to remember your belovedness in that place.

Day 16

IDENTIFYING IN CHRIST

*I have been crucified with Christ. It is no longer I who
live, but Christ who lives in me. And the life I now live
in the flesh I live by faith in the Son of God, who loved
me and gave himself for me. (Galatians 2:20 ESV)*

So much of our anxiety is tied to trying to prevent, manage, or
avoid pain. This is understandable! It's very human to not like
pain.

One of the beautiful things about Jesus is that he not only
knows pain intimately but also *redeems* pain. He doesn't ignore,
reframe, or try to explain pain. Instead, he *enters into it.* He experienced the most excruciating, humiliating death imaginable *for
our sake.* Then he rose, bringing light from darkness. He *moved*
from death to life.

We see this same pattern in our passage today. Paul stated
that he had *died* with Christ. Since Paul was alive when he wrote
this, he was saying that his sin and shame had been put to death
with Christ on the cross. This means nothing flawed or broken in
him had the final say over his life or identity. Nor did his pain.
Paul was declaring he was not defined by his brokenness; he was
defined *by Christ living in him.* He was identifying in Christ.

When we put our faith in Jesus, we are united to Christ by the
Holy Spirit. Our lives become forever linked with the One whose
suffering and death *lead to* beauty and meaning. The backward
pattern of death to life becomes *our* pattern. We die to our sin
(turning away from it and back to Jesus) over and over. In these
daily ways, we join Jesus in his death and then his resurrection.

We experience other types of death in this pattern as well.
Failure, losses, disappointments, and rejection can all be ways we
share in the suffering of Christ (Philippians 3:10). For me, this
has been friendships that have faded. Hopes to be asked out that

53

have been dashed. Injuries that have stolen my ability to play sports. Negative feedback that has unraveled my best efforts.

The pain of these deaths is very real—whether they are due to our sin, others' sin against us, or sin's impact on the created world. And *these are the places* where the Lord meets us compassionately. He honors the full weight of our brokenness and our suffering.

But we also remember that *in Christ*, the Holy Spirit carries us *through these deaths* to resurrections. Christ *redeems* our pain. Because he died and rose again, death can never be the end of the story.

Little resurrections pepper my life in ways I wouldn't expect.

When I repent of specific sins, I experience relief and freedom from enslavement to shame. My heart softens toward those who struggle with the same thing.

When I experience failure, loss, or disappointment, my resilience grows. I learn that the Lord will see me through even the most painful times. I also grow in love toward those who've experienced similar hurt. My faith in God's ability to provide hope, comfort, and peace increases. My eyesight for glory also grows; I am primed and ready to spot even the smallest joys and beauties around me.

Our Lord died to *redeem all the brokenness* in us and this world. And our Lord rose that love might work its way into every crevice of creation. As we join him in the pattern of death and resurrection, we remember that our pain does not define us. Christ does. He is the one who makes beauty from pain.

> Breathe in: *I am not defined by my sin or pain.*
> Breathe out: *I am defined by Christ.*
>
> Where are you currently sharing in the death of Christ? When is a time you have experienced a resurrection in, with, or through him?

Day 17

HEIRS OF THE KING

Now if we are children, then we are heirs—heirs of God and co-heirs with Christ, if indeed we share in his sufferings in order that we may also share in his glory. (Romans 8:17)

In days 15 and 16, we explored what it means to be children of God and to suffer with Christ. Today, we get to wonder at the glory of being heirs of God—an influential and dignified role that infuses our lives with purpose.

I vividly remember the anxiety of entering high school. I feared being at the bottom of the food chain. Who would my people be? Would anyone want me in their group?

Who we are associated with holds a great deal of power. We identify ourselves with different famous people, sports teams, political parties, and interest groups that fit our leanings. We long to *be on the inside*. We desire to be *seen* and *recognized*.

In the story of Narnia, one of the children, Edmund, had this same desire. Although he acted like he didn't care, he secretly longed to *matter*. He imagined status would give him meaning and security. In fact, he went so far as to betray his siblings to the evil White Witch in exchange for her promise to make him an heir to her throne.

Things didn't go well for Edmund, and he ended up being taken hostage by the White Witch. He gave deference and allegiance to the wrong person, and he became enslaved to her. The promise of a royal identity transformed into oppressive shackles instead.

Edmund's story is a picture of what happened in the garden. Adam and Eve were originally created to serve as honored, royal caretakers of God's world. But they decided they wanted to be their own king and queen. They wanted royalty on their own terms. They wanted to make a name for themselves instead of associating with God's name, so they became shackled to sin.

The rest of the story of Scripture reveals God's plan to reinstate Adam and Eve as his royal children. He wanted them to know the blessing of being in *his* family. He longed for them to be ruled by his love and not by lesser things.

With the voice that created the heavens and the earth, he declares us *heirs of the kingdom* in Christ. In fact, he *places his name on us*, saying, *"This one's mine. I associate with this person."* And in doing this, he bestows a title of dignity, beauty, and authority on us. This status is given—not bought, achieved, or earned. This royal relationship is *secured*, because it is based on Christ's completed work and not ours.

As sons and daughters of King Jesus, we are forever enfolded into a story where *we matter*. We receive an inheritance of honor, never-ceasing grace, and open access to the Holy Spirit, who helps us to steward our power and reminds us of who we truly are.

Here's how this looked in Narnia: After king Aslan sacrificed himself to break Edmund's shackles, Edmund got to spend the rest of his life learning to *live into* his status as a beloved, royal son. With the title "King Edmund the Just" bestowed on him, he received all the rights and privileges of being brought into the king's family. He then began to steward the power he was given—his God-given heart for justice—to love and serve others. As you consider the domain the Lord has given you—whether that's a school, a team, a family, or something else—how might you lovingly steward the royalty and power King Jesus has uniquely bestowed on you?

Breathe in: *Even when I fear I don't matter—*
Breathe out: *I am an heir of the King.*

In Narnia, the children were given titles they learned to live into (King Peter the Magnificent, Queen Susan the Gentle, and Queen Lucy the Valiant). What title would you be given?

BELONGING IN THE BODY OF CHRIST

*Just as a body, though one, has many parts, but all its
many parts form one body, so it is with Christ. For we
were all baptized by one Spirit so as to form one body—
whether Jews or Gentiles, slave or free—and we were all
given the one Spirit to drink. (1 Corinthians 12:12–13)*

One of our great sources of anxiety comes from worrying that we don't have a place. We don't belong. We aren't wanted. We don't have anything valuable to contribute.

This is when it becomes a blessing and relief to remember that our truth comes from outside us. No matter how weakly you *believe* that you matter and that you belong to the body of Christ, God's Word declares that you are essential. Something important is missing when you are missing from the body of Christ! You are needed.

As believers in Christ, we are not only united to God through the Holy Spirit. We are also united to the people of God. We become a part of his family—a family that spans the entire globe and all of history. We are linked together by something far more powerful than a shared interest or cause. It is even more enduring than the blood we share with our genetic parents. God himself causes us to belong. His love serves as the glue that holds us fast in his body. Christ is the head, and we are the parts that make up the body. Every single part is needed—especially the weaker and more vulnerable parts (1 Corinthians 12:21). Although we might worry we have nothing to offer or are too much of a burden, God's Word is clear: we are necessary. Our voices, our struggles, our gifts, our perspectives, and our questions are needed.

I used to volunteer with a youth group (called Capernaum) for teenagers with Down syndrome. I don't know if I've ever had so much fun! First, everyone would walk into a victory tunnel of cheering and high fives. Then we'd all sit down for dinner together and listen to a Bible message. Finally, we'd have an all-out dance party. The shyest and most self-conscious teenage volunteers would be led out onto the dance floor by the warmest and most joyful smiles of the Capernaum kids. It was truly a taste of heaven.

We *all* have something valuable to offer in the body of Christ. Sometimes we offer our hands in service, like the volunteers did. And sometimes we offer hospitality with welcoming smiles and hugs, like my Capernaum friends did. Sometimes we offer our humor and sometimes our sadness. Sometimes we offer our ears to listen and sometimes our stories to be heard. Sometimes we offer our honest doubts, and sometimes we offer reminders of how God has shown up in our lives. All these are vital in the body of Christ.

We live in a world that says our value is in our independence and our strengths. It's terrible and undesirable to be "needy."

But we also live in the family of God, where *needy* is our starting point. It isn't shameful. It's a reality that takes courage to acknowledge. Christians recognize that we need help. We need rescue. We need God to enter in—time and again—to infuse us with his truth. And we need one another—to share in burden-bearing, grief, joy, and beauty. We need someone to lead us out onto the dance floor!

There's freedom in knowing we don't have to pretend. We're all needy. In fact, our needs are needed in the body of Christ because God has designed us to depend on one another. This means every gift matters and every need matters. No matter what lie your anxiety is telling today, you belong. And you are needed.

Breathe in: *When I feel needy—*
Breathe out: *My needs belong in the body of Christ.*

When is a time you were blessed by someone allowing you to care for their needs? What are some things that keep us from sharing our needs with the body of Christ?

SAFE TO STRUGGLE IN OUR LORD

*I do not understand what I do. For what I want to do I do not do,
but what I hate I do.... What a wretched man I am! Who will rescue
me from this body that is subject to death? Thanks be to God, who
delivers me through Jesus Christ our Lord! (Romans 7:15, 24–25)*

My golden retriever Bo Diddley was the most mischievous, fun-loving dude you could ever imagine. He greeted every stranger he met with a goofy grin. He also stole every undefended food item he could. Tomatoes, butter, and apples were his favorites.

One afternoon when I was in grad school, I walked out of my room to find a completely intact, packaged, frozen T-bone steak in the middle of my living room floor. I was confused until I saw Bo cowering in his hiding spot behind a chair. His head was down, and he had those upturned guilty eyes I'd come to know so well.

All I could do was laugh. Evidently my roommate had left her dinner to defrost on the counter before running an errand. Bo had done what he knew he wasn't supposed to do. However, somewhere in the middle of his steak heist, he was overtaken by a sense of conviction. He was the picture of Paul's internal battle in Romans 7.

Anxiety can have a number of sources. *Nature* (such as personality or biological predispositions), *nurture* (such as family and social dynamics), *context* (such as season of the school year, conflict in a relationship, and so on) and *past trauma* can all come into play. Conviction can as well. Our desire to *want* to do what is right can generate anxiety.

For me, Paul's struggle makes Romans 7 one of the most relatable chapters in the whole Bible. Here was a Christian who loved the Lord, yet he was wrestling with the question "Why do I do the things I'm *not* supposed to do, and why don't I do the things I *am* supposed to do?" Paul was caught in the war of his sin and his conscience (where the Holy Spirit was at work). He was frustrated. And his battle builds throughout the chapter, culminating with an exasperated declaration: "What a wretched man I am!"

We can trace the pattern of Paul's thoughts in verses 24–25: they are oriented inward, then outward and upward.

In Paul's *inward* segment, we read the back-and-forth of his thoughts. He wrestled honestly with himself, asking questions and responding to them. He then moved *outward*, presenting a desperate question: "Who will rescue me from this body that is subject to death?" Finally, he moved *upward* toward God, giving thanks as he remembered the deliverance of Jesus. We find conviction, confession, and assurance of pardon. The sold-out-for-Jesus author of thirteen books of the New Testament shows us we are safe to struggle in our Lord.

Sometimes when I can't figure out what is sin, what is anxiety, and what is legitimate conviction, I hold my hands to my chest as I go *inward*. I wrestle back and forth, praying for clarity and discernment. Then I lay my hands open with my palms up on my lap, mentally placing the whole mess of thoughts and emotions in that space (*outward*). I raise my hands *upward*, offering the Lord everything there and receiving his reminder: "It is finished. You are forgiven. You are my beloved daughter, and you're safe with me." Thanks be to God in Jesus Christ, there is now no condemnation for those of us who put our faith in Christ (Romans 8:1). Absolutely nothing—including our inability to figure it out or get it right—can separate us from his love (Romans 8:38).

Breathe in: *Who will rescue me in this battle?*
Breathe out: *Thanks be to God in Jesus Christ.*

What battle are you having with yourself right now? Take a couple minutes to try using your hands and body to offer this battle to the Lord and receive his grace afresh.

Day 20

COURAGE TO BE VULNERABLE

Going a little farther, he fell to the ground and prayed that if possible the hour might pass from him. "Abba, Father," he said, "everything is possible for you. Take this cup from me. Yet not what I will, but what you will." (Mark 14:35–36)

In today's passage, Jesus was in the garden of Gethsemane. He was about to be betrayed by his friend Judas. He was struggling. He didn't have the posture of a confident hero going into battle. He knew that he was about to be brutally executed, and he let this reality impact his heart. Mark 14:33 tells us he was deeply distressed and troubled. Jesus was overwhelmed with sorrow and anguish—even to the point where he sweated blood (Luke 22:44). Here in the garden, Jesus was vulnerable.

Anxiety can make me feel similarly vulnerable. And when I feel vulnerable, I tend to get tough. I don't want other people to think I need help. I don't want to burden anyone. I want to figure it out on my own. Yet isolation tends to make things worse.

Research has shown that healing and change require vulnerability. When you scraped your knee as a kid, you had to reveal that scrape to your mom so she could clean it out. Vulnerability was letting your mom see and tend to your wound. It required risk and letting down your guard. When we struggle with anxiety, shame, or other types of internal pain, the same is true. Healing comes partially through revealing what is *inside us* to someone safe and trusted. We must risk letting someone else *see* and *love* us.

It is helpful for me to remember that the God of the world *made* himself vulnerable in his own anxious distress. In a moment of profound honesty, he fell to the ground, desperately calling out to his Father.

It is scary to risk being vulnerable. But Jesus found courage in who God is. With "Abba," he recognized God as his

61

compassionate Father. With "everything is possible for you," he recognized God as his sovereign King. Remembering God's love and his power made Jesus brave. He prayed an incredibly vulnerable prayer: "Take this cup from me." *Please take this burden, God. Please change these circumstances. I know you are able to do it.*

There's an air of desperation to Jesus's request. He knew his Father cared so deeply for him that he could cry out wholeheartedly. Then he offered his desire to trust: *Yet not what I will, but what you will.* His neediness did not make him faithless. And his faith did not belittle his need. He let the two exist in tension.

It takes a great deal of courage to be as honest as Jesus is here. But I bet he didn't *feel* courageous. Courage is doing the scary thing. Often asking for help from others or from God feels embarrassing and nerve-wracking. It requires the risk of burdening someone or receiving an answer that might not be what we want to hear.

In this case, God did *not* take Jesus's burden. His ultimate story of love involved using that very burden (Jesus's own death) to bless the world. If God does not remove your struggle, you are in good company. Jesus himself knew what that was like.

In my experience, the Christian life involves far more *redeeming* of burdens than *delivery* of burdens. God can certainly do both: he can *use* our struggles for good, and he can *remove* our struggles altogether. Only he knows truly what is best. One thing we know for sure is that love is always his goal. None of our struggles is wasted as he shapes us more into people who vulnerably give and receive love.

Breathe in: *When I am tempted to keep my anxiety to myself—*
Breathe out: *Give me courage to be vulnerable, Lord.*

What are some of the things that keep you from sharing vulnerably with God? From sharing vulnerably with others?

WELCOMED IN OUR WRESTLING

Although the doors were locked, Jesus came and stood among them and said, "Peace be with you." Then he said to Thomas, "Put your finger here, and see my hands; and put out your hand, and place it in my side. Do not disbelieve, but believe." (John 20:26–27 ESV)

Recently, a dear friend described an experience of extreme anxiety to me. His hands felt like they were on fire, and adrenaline shot through his body. His mind and body felt almost entirely out of control. He began battling with God. "Where are you? Are you even there?" "How can you be good if you allow things like this to happen?" "How can I believe you love me when you let me go through this?"

Often when we experience significant powerlessness or loss of control (as with a death, an accident, a breakup, a physical condition, abuse, or something else), we are left with big questions for God.

In John 20, we read about the doubt of one of Jesus's disciples. Thomas had just lost one of his closest friends, and he was wrestling with his faith. He may very well have been asking the same questions my friend did. He was understandably upset and skeptical. Not only did he mistrust what Jesus had told him (Matthew 20:17–19), but he was cynical about the other disciples' claim that Jesus had risen from the dead. In John 20:25, Thomas essentially said, "Prove it. Unless I see and touch Jesus's wounds, I won't believe it."

One of the more freeing realities of the Christian faith is how often we read about God's beloved people wrestling with his goodness and with who he is. They wrestle in their suffering, as Paul did with his thorn (2 Corinthians 12:7). They wrestle in their grief, as Martha did when her brother Lazarus died (John 11:21).

And they wrestle in their longings, which we read about in many places (most especially in the Psalms). Christianity is not a faith for people who know all the answers and have it all together. It's a faith for those who grow in dependence on Jesus, whose gracious welcome extends to all our questions. Honest Christianity lives at the intersection of faith and doubt.

Let's slow down to consider how Jesus dealt with doubting people in John 20.

First, we see him move *toward* his people intentionally, as he went to the place where they'd gathered. He offered them comfort with the words "Peace be with you."

The next thing Jesus did is worth a pause. Did he shame Thomas for his doubts? Did he lecture him? Did he ignore his question? No: Jesus accepted Thomas's doubt and moved toward *him* specifically—both in heart and in body. He offered himself vulnerably for Thomas to interact with. He invited Thomas to touch his crucifixion scars, welcoming Thomas to engage his doubt.

Jesus doesn't stay distant when we struggle with questions that arise from our experiences of powerlessness. He draws near in the Holy Spirit.

God created you intentionally with a body, and he is currently upholding the complex workings of every part. Place your fingers on your wrist and find your pulse. *Feel* the blood pumping through your veins. The King is sustaining you. He faced powerlessness himself on the cross so that you might never again face powerlessness on your own. He's given you his body of believers and the Holy Spirit to bear your struggles with you. He lovingly welcomes all your wrestling. He invites every question you've got.

Breathe in: *When I'm wrestling—*
Breathe out: *Jesus offers me his body.*

What is one of your big questions right now? Who is someone in the body of Christ you can imagine sharing that question with?

GOD HOLDS US TOGETHER

The Son is the image of the invisible God, the firstborn over all creation. For in him all things were created: things in heaven and on earth, visible and invisible, whether thrones or powers or rulers or authorities; all things have been created through him and for him. He is before all things, and in him all things hold together. (Colossians 1:15–17)

Today, I drove six hours from Tennessee to Virginia with my sick dog in the car.

I had been dreading this drive.

My back has been spasming for the last week. This means driving is particularly painful right now.

My mind has been cycling on a particular conflict I'm having with a friend. This means alone time is overwhelming right now because my thoughts have free rein to assault me.

I'm heading toward time with my family. This means stress is likely.

What does it mean that God is holding all things together when it feels like they are falling apart?

I asked my friends at my Bible study that question this morning. We opened to the above verses in Colossians. In this passage, we read that God created all things in the Son. He created sunshine and oxygen, heartbeats and gravity. He crafted the intricacies of atoms and molecules and the mysteries of love and beauty. Abraham Kuyper wrote that "there is not a square inch in the whole domain of our human existence over which Christ, who is Sovereign over all, does not cry: 'Mine!'"[1]

My friends and I brainstormed real-world metaphors together. Like God, the director of a play knows the ins and outs of every scene, every script, and every transition. The conductor of an orchestra keeps the rhythm of each song and is aware of each instrument's part. A farmer keeps track of soil, seasons, and crops while tending the plants daily. And a good parent holds you tight in a bear hug when you're coming undone. In all these ways, we see sustaining. Maintaining. Stewardship. Intimate involvement.

Yet our God is even greater than any of these. The Creator-Sustainer of the entire universe never takes a break. Never misses a beat. Never fails to see our tears. He is present even in our longing for him to show up. Our desire for relief and healing is a sign he is at work. His love never stops coming for us.

So let me share how that looked for me today.

About five hours into my drive, I noticed my back wasn't feeling as angry as I thought it would. I was so grateful! I began to wonder at the other ways God had sustained me. At that moment in my drive, a podcast on chronic pain held my full attention. Earlier, an audiobook entertained me. A playlist served up countless songs to sing to. A back cushion supported my spine. Beautiful mountains captured my imagination. My dog smiled her usual smile even though she wasn't well. A friend texted that she was praying for me. I evaded a crazy driver and avoided an accident. In all these things, God held me together. He met me with the reminder of his intimate sovereignty. It's not that he removed any of the factors that made me feel like my world was falling apart. Instead, he helped to starve my worry by feeding my wonder at his provision. He opened my eyes to how his love was coming at me.

Breathe in: *When it feels like things are falling apart—*
Breathe out: *God is holding all things together.*

Spend some time wondering. What are some ways God sustained you today (or yesterday)?

CONNECTION ENJOYED

"Courage is not the absence of anxiety but the practice of trusting that we will be held and loved no matter what happens."
K. J. Ramsey, This Too Shall Last

The Christian story is one of relentless pursuit by our God—a constant welcome (and welcome back) into relationship with him. God initiates over and over, inviting us to turn to him, to trust in him. He desires for his love to extend to every part of our hearts, minds, and bodies—and this world. Over and over, he reminds us there is nothing we can do to make him love us more, and there is nothing we can do to make him love us less. He loves us perfectly. Our faith is dependent on what *he* has done, not on anything that we do.

Yet God does not leave us as he finds us. He meets us in every deep, dark, anxious corner of our lives, and he offers us more. He offers us his Spirit as we learn to live as his beloved children.

When I adopted my dog, Bella, she had only ever lived in a kennel. She hadn't been raised in a world with a lot of rules or a lot of cuddles. She was walked twice a day and bred twice a year, and she loved any attention she was given.

I brought her home for a "trial weekend" a couple months ago. She nervously walked around the house for a while. Then she sat on the floor and looked to me for guidance. What next? Well, I sat on the couch and let her jump up and throw her seventy-pound body onto my lap. Then we snuggled for a good long time. Within a very short while, I knew she was to be mine. I was to be her human, and she was to be my creature. I went out and bought her a collar and a tag that said *Bella Edrington*. I put my name on her. Now she is learning to be mine. And in that she's learning to be a beloved pet.

There is nothing Bella could do to make me love her any less. Sometimes her behaviors scare or worry me, but that doesn't change my deep affection for her. It wouldn't have been loving for me to adopt her and then leave *her* to figure out how to live life with me. She looks to me to *learn* to be mine. And I get to teach her how to flourish—how to enjoy being the creature God has created her to be. This means she is learning to play with tennis balls. She is learning to "stay." She is learning all manner of things about what it means to be a pet.

This is similar for us: we are completely secured in the love of God, who has adopted us into his family. He set his seal on us (2 Corinthians 1:22). And now we get to learn to enjoy that connection. We get to learn to live as humans have been *created* to live. We are *becoming* the people he's created us to be, more and more. Just as Bella is learning to trust me more and more to guide her into being a beloved pet, we are learning to trust Jesus more and more. We are learning to be his beloved, dependent children who participate in his grand story of filling the earth with his love.

RECEIVING DAILY BREAD

*Then Jesus declared, "I am the bread of life. Whoever
comes to me will never go hungry, and whoever
believes in me will never be thirsty." (John 6:35)*

God loves bodies.

I know. It sounds weird. But stick with me.

Our bodies are a battlefield for our anxiety. They blush. They
get hives. They tense up. They crackle with energy. They tingle.
They go numb. They become nauseous. Sometimes it seems like
our bodies are the enemy.

But the Creator of the universe himself took on a body that
was able to feel all those things. Jesus didn't skip over the hard
parts of having a body. He was hungry. He needed sleep. He went
through puberty. He experienced pain. He can empathize with
our discomfort.

Jesus also drew near to the Father with his body. He held
the Scriptures in his hands. He opened his mouth in prayer. He
removed himself from people to commune with God. He received
bodily care in the form of food, foot washing, and the loving presence of others.

Jesus showed us that our bodies are a huge part of how we
receive God every day.

In our reading today, we heard him say something pretty wild.
He declared that he is the Bread of Life. He was speaking to a
massive crowd of people whom he'd fed the day before with just
two fish and five loaves of bread. When they'd gathered that day,
he hadn't just preached to them. He'd tended to their bodily needs.
He'd acknowledged the hunger in their bellies and provided for
them. "They had eaten their fill," John says in 6:12 (ESV).

So on this day when he claimed that he *is* the Bread of
Life, the people would remember that Jesus had fed them the

day before. The taste of freshly cooked fish and dry, chewy bread would pop into their minds. They would recall opening their hands to receive that sustenance. They would tie together their experience of fullness and satisfaction with this huge statement: "I am the Bread of Life."

This is not the statement of a mere teacher. This is the statement of a Lord. This is an invitation to receive the mystery of God's grace every day. It is the reminder that *he* is the one who—like bread—sustains. He has more than just information for his people. He offers *himself* as our provision each day, and we get to trust him to provide for tomorrow.

King Jesus, the Bread of Life, is a never-ending meal. He nourishes our embodied souls in countless ways—whether through easing our anxiety, giving us perseverance for the day, sparking hope for the future, or offering companionship as he grieves our painful experiences with us. He longs for us to feast on him.

When we get caught up in anxiety over what will happen tomorrow, we can look for ways the Lord is inviting us to receive his grace with our bodies today. We can receive him through the truths our eyes take in as we read the Word of God. We can receive him through each bite of tasty food and drink that satisfies us. We can receive him through the music that tickles our ears and delights our souls. We can receive him through the warmth of the sun on our skin and the comfort of a hug from a friend. God's broken body on our behalf means there is always more of the grace of Jesus to receive.

Breathe in: *My body is not the enemy.*
Breathe out: *It is a receiver of the Bread of Life.*

What is one way you can receive the grace offered through the Bread of Life with your body today?

HONORING OUR LIMITS

I am the gate; whoever enters through me will be saved.
They will come in and go out, and find pasture. The thief
comes only to steal and kill and destroy; I have come that
they may have life, and have it to the full. (John 10:9–10)

Recently, I've been watching a cheesy Canadian TV show called *Heartland*. The story follows families who own horses, ranches, and cattle (and experience lots of drama, as you'd expect). I've learned that when you own cows, one of the most important things you have to do is maintain the fencing. If a fence is damaged or broken, the cows can escape and any number of bad things can happen. They can be stolen or fall down ravines. They can be injured by wild animals. The fencing is a critical part of the cows' thriving.

We live in a world that tells us that fencing is oppressive and limitlessness is freedom. We now have limitless gender options. Information access through the internet seems limitless. Menus for restaurants read like novels. We're told we would truly be free if we could throw off whatever is preventing us from following our hearts.

But what if this picture of freedom is actually fueling our anxiety? What if limitlessness isn't actually good for us?

In our reading today, Jesus referred to himself as the gate of a sheep pen. Similar to the *Heartland* fences, a sheep pen protected the animals at night, allowing them to rest safely as their shepherd guarded against predators such as wolves. The shepherd's goodness and trustworthiness meant the pen's limits were life-giving, not freedom-taking.

The same is true for humans. We find true rest and freedom from anxiety when we honor the good limits God has created. Some of these are external limits like the Ten Commandments.

If we all followed them—loving and respecting God and one another—the world would be a much more beautiful place. Other limits are internal needs. Even the perfect person of Jesus needed food, rest, and companionship. He wasn't a robot.

Our Good Shepherd didn't intend for us to work for twenty-four hours of the day, to have all the knowledge in the world, or to possess the unique gifts of our friends. He didn't intend for us to be good at everything or to have energy for every possible event. He created us with limits—and the need for limits—that help us to flourish. Although we often become frustrated when we bump up against our limits, God is working *within* our limits. For example, the physical limit of our need for sleep is not going away. But God may be healing the way we think and feel about rest (which helps us thrive!).

For me, honoring my limits can look like saying no to hanging out when I don't have the energy. It can look like closing my laptop at 5 p.m. instead of obsessively perfecting my work. It can look like calling a friend for support when I can't get my anxious mind to turn off. It can look like clarifying what I'm actually feeling when someone else makes an assumption about what I'm feeling.

One thing is for sure: I always need to be reminded of the good limits God has given for my flourishing. When I open the Word of God, the lies of my anxiety are corralled by truths of who I am in Christ. Here I am led by a truly Good Shepherd instead of by my wandering heart. In him, we find healing for all the ways we resist our limits as we try to live on our own terms apart from God. In him, we find life to the full.

Breathe in: *I am limited—*
Breathe out: *By the intentional design of the Good Shepherd.*

Often, we are frustrated or embarrassed by our good, God-given limits. What is one limit the Lord might be inviting you to honor rather than to view with shame?

Day 25

RESTING WITH JESUS

*"Martha, Martha," the Lord answered, "you are worried and
upset about many things, but few things are needed—
or indeed only one. Mary has chosen what is better, and
it will not be taken away from her." (Luke 10:41–42)*

"You are worried and upset about many things." What an accurate statement about my life. It's like Jesus is calling *me* out along with Martha.

But Jesus never calls people out with the end goal of shaming them or making fun of them. He calls them out to invite them to experience more of his grace. He calls them to rest in himself.

There are few people in the Bible I can relate to as much as Martha.

I imagine her as a bit of an eager beaver. She readily opened her home to Jesus (Luke 10:38). She wanted him to have a wonderful experience. So she began tidying and organizing. She prepared food to eat. She bustled about with a giant checklist of things to do in order to be a good hostess. Her desire to serve well quickly overshadowed the one she was serving. Her eyes shifted to all she wanted to get done instead of the One who was lovingly waiting to be with her.

I wonder if Martha's busyness was anything like mine. My busyness can be both a source and a byproduct of my anxiety. In high school, I had every hour of the day scheduled with school, Bible studies, sports practices, and homework. My life was driven by "good" things, but those good things were also a huge source of stress. If I had a little gap in my schedule, my anxiety would cause me to Martha about, finding various tasks to complete— anything to distract me or bring a sense of accomplishment.

There are plenty of reasons Martha may have been running around like a chicken with her head cut off. If she was like me, it was probably easier for her to be a human *doing* rather than a human *being*. I'm betting she too felt a sense of power in completing tasks. She too could avoid loneliness and disappointment by filling her schedule.

Yet here in Luke 10, we're given the picture of a better way. It isn't necessarily the *easier* way (even though it seems like it should be). But it is better. Jesus disrupted Martha's anxious busyness with the invitation to rest in his presence.

Let's first note the *way* Jesus disrupts. After gently interrupting Martha by using her name, Jesus acknowledged her reality. He *saw* her. He could tell she was anxious about many things, and he reflected this to her. He lovingly held up a mirror to her, inviting her to see that her busyness wasn't working for her.

Then he pointed her to Mary. In verse 39, we learn that Mary was sitting at the Lord's feet listening to him. We don't know Mary's motivation. We aren't told about her struggles. It's possible that she was even more anxious than Martha.

What we do know is that Mary put her body in a position to rest in God's presence. With everything going on in her life, she paused and opened her ears to listen to him.

Mary may very well have had a difficult time leaving her own tasks to sit with Jesus. But she still turned from those tasks and lowered herself to the floor. She placed her body in a position that helped her to pay attention to Jesus. She prioritized listening to the One who could remind her of her belovedness, teach her about her purpose, and give her faith in his sovereignty. He could offer her better relief than task completion could. Mary used her body and ears to help her rest in Jesus's presence.

Breathe in: *When I am worried and upset by many things*—
Breathe out: *Jesus invites me to rest at his feet.*

What is a way you can use your body and ears to rest in God's presence today? For example, try walking in a beautiful place while listening to music that praises God.

RELEASING OUR NEED TO KNOW

The Spirit helps us in our weakness. We do not know what we ought to pray for, but the Spirit himself intercedes for us through wordless groans. And he who searches our hearts knows the mind of the Spirit, because the Spirit intercedes for God's people in accordance with the will of God. (Romans 8:26–27)

We all have intrusive thoughts—unwanted thoughts or images that pop into our minds. It may be the fear of something bad happening or it may be a distressing idea that you want out of your brain. Most of the time, these thoughts fly into our awareness like birds into a tree, and then they fly right back out. But sometimes one gets stuck in the branches. It loops around and around. When this happens, telling ourselves to stop thinking about it doesn't work.

To demonstrate how the mind works, let's try something: I want you to *not think about* a pink elephant.

What happened? You immediately conjured up the image of a gigantic, rosy-trunked beast, didn't you?

It can be hard to even know how to pray when a thought is on repeat. This is when we need help from the outside—like our verse today says, someone to intercede for us.

I had one of these moments last month. I had just attended my fifty-fifth wedding since college. I have always wanted to be married, so although I was very happy for my friends, I was left with great surges of sadness, anger, and loneliness when I came home. The thought on repeat was "I'm never going to be married. It's always the same for me."

I've learned in these looping moments that I have to get moving. So I threw myself out the door and onto my bike, full of pent-up everything. As I pedaled with fury, I can remember thinking, "Lord, I don't even know how to pray right now." So I aimed my emotions at him and wordlessly brought him everything I had.

In my mind, I can still see where I was on the trail when the Holy Spirit intervened. It wasn't an amazing eureka moment. It was a simple memory that floated into my mind: In my late teens, I thought I'd lost biking forever when it began causing me to have awful back spasms. But in my thirties, God returned biking to me. With that reminder from the Spirit, gratitude filled my heart. I began confessing to God all the things I *didn't actually know* (because I thought I'd *known* I'd never bike again).

"I don't know that I'll never run again. I don't know that I'll never be married. I don't know that I won't own a kayak one day." God's thoughts are higher than our thoughts, and his ways are not our ways (Isaiah 55:8–9).

I often unconsciously believe life would be better *if I just knew* my future. My mind cycles and cycles, trying to figure it out. But God is the one who *actually knows* what will come to pass. And he has surprised me on more than one occasion.

He is also the one who guarantees that my story will have a redemptive ending, no matter how stuck I can get on a certain assumption, prediction, fear, or memory.

I wish I could say that I'd set out with holy intentions to bring my heart before the Lord on that bike ride. But the reality is that the Spirit met me in my weakness. I simply got onto that bike and began pouring myself out to God. Looking back, I see now that the Spirit was searching my heart, looking out for me, and praying for me (interceding). He met me right where he knew I needed meeting. He was helping me release what I *thought I knew*. He was helping me trust him with my *need to know*.

Breathe in: *When I am stuck in my need to know—*
Breathe out: *The Spirit intercedes for me.*

Make a list to practice releasing what you think you know to the Lord. "Jesus, I don't know _____."

GIVING OUR ALLEGIANCE TO KING JESUS

Whoever fears the Lᴏʀᴅ has a secure fortress, and for their children it will be a refuge. The fear of the Lᴏʀᴅ is a fountain of life, turning a person from the snares of death. (Proverbs 14:26–27)

Human fear is a powerful thing. It often lurks beneath the surface without our even realizing it. We get mad at a friend when they don't invite us to hang out (we're afraid they don't actually like us). We act like we don't care when no one asks us out (we're afraid there's something wrong with us). We procrastinate or obsess over assignments (we're afraid of failure). We play down our desire to make the team, get the callback, or go to a particular college (we're afraid we'll be rejected).

Fear rarely feels good. But it isn't a bad thing. Like any emotion, it tells us about something important happening in our story. And it can help us to be curious about what that is. For example, one time my dog ran away, and I was terrified she'd be hit by a car. This fear told me I cared deeply about Bella. Another time, my doctor told me my kidneys weren't working properly. I was scared my diagnosis could mean a shortened life. This fear told me I cared deeply about living.

Tim Keller wrote, "'Fear' in the Bible means to be overwhelmed, to be controlled by something."[1] The things we fear hold a lot of controlling power in our lives. This power grows when we avoid these things or center our worry on them. We have to catch ourselves in the process of fearing. For me, this often involves asking the Holy Spirit and a friend, "What am I afraid of right now?"

Then I get to hold that fear up to the only one who actually deserves my fear: King Jesus. Only with him can fear lead to *security* and to a *fountain of life*. This is because there is no fear over which he is not sovereign. There is no fear his love cannot reach into. He has the ultimate power over every single matter in our lives. Because he is ruling from his throne, we can play our fears out to their fullest extent and let his truths speak into them. We can practice giving our allegiance to our good King instead of to our fears.

This can look like confessing to a friend and asking for prayer: "I know this sounds crazy, but I've been feeling lonely, and I think I fear that no one really likes me. Would you pray for me?"

This can look like writing down a list of fears and then searching for how God's Word addresses them: "I fear I am unlovable" → "I have loved you with an everlasting love; I have drawn you with unfailing kindness" (Jeremiah 31:3).

This can look like acknowledging our fear and then turning our attention to our Creator's greatness. Where do you experience wonder at his beauty? What helps you turn the volume up on his majesty? My endlessly creative friend Elissa does this by going on "contemplative color walks." First, she chooses a specific color (something like fuchsia), then as she goes for a walk, she scans her surroundings to find the color. It could be a flower. It could be a candy wrapper. She snaps a picture any time she finds something. She allows her imagination to be captured by the Lord's glorious gift of fuchsia.

Our God never dismisses our fears. Instead, he invites us to bring them to him. He is far more worthy of our allegiance. With him, we get to let ourselves be overwhelmed by his glorious grace.

Breathe in: *My fear is powerful.*
Breathe out: *But not as powerful as King Jesus.*

What is one way you want to practice giving your allegiance to King Jesus instead of to your fear today?

Day 28

REMEMBERING THE UPSIDE-DOWN KINGDOM

Three times I pleaded with the Lord to take [my thorn] away from me. But he said to me, "My grace is sufficient for you, for my power is made perfect in weakness." Therefore I will boast all the more gladly about my weaknesses, so that Christ's power may rest on me. (2 Corinthians 12:8–9)

Some anxiety sparks in little bursts that wear themselves out in an hour or two. Some lingers for weeks at a time. And some anxiety clings like a fog that just won't lift. It's a lot like chronic pain.

Not long ago, I had some pain in my left foot that wouldn't go away. I went to an orthopedic doctor who casually held my X-rays up and said, "Oh yeah. I don't even know how you're walking on that thing. You're never going to run or play soccer again."

I was devastated, to say the least. Soccer had been my passion for my whole life. Running had also been important for managing seasons of depression. This was a real type of death for me.

In day 16, we saw that death to life is a regular pattern in Christianity. In God's kingdom, things don't work like they do in the world. Jesus doesn't crush his enemies through brute strength. He disarms them through humility, gentleness, and suffering, dying for us on the cross. In Jesus's upside-down kingdom, weakness and dependence are more valuable than might.

In the reading today, Paul describes how he pleaded with the Lord to take away his chronic thorn. We don't know what he was struggling with; we just know it was so disruptive that he begged God to take it away. God invites us to ask him for big things. If you're like me, you have begged God to take away your chronic condition.

In Scripture, we see that sometimes God delivered his people from chronic conditions like infertility, bleeding, blindness, and leprosy. But more often he delivered his people *through* their chronic conditions. Instead of removing the difficulty, he met them *in* their weakness and grief—and he meets us in the same way. He has compassion for us (Psalm 145:8–9). He weeps with us (John 11:35). He provides grace just as we need it. This is where we experience the upside-down kingdom. Although our world works through strength and success, our God works through powerlessness and death (2 Corinthians 12:9).

God's upside-down kingdom makes very little worldly sense, and it hinges entirely on the gospel. If the life, death, and resurrection of Jesus aren't true, our suffering is meaningless and feeling good in this life is the best we can hope for. But Jesus offers us more: he offers us the chance to *experience* and *witness* his kingdom in our pain. His grace meets us in surprising ways around every dark corner. He makes beauty from suffering.

The thing is, our chronic thorns still *feel* like death. My foot still hurts daily. It is a cross I bear, just as chronic anxiety may be a cross for you (Matthew 16:24).

But the mystery of Christ is this: death does not have the final say. The upside-down kingdom *is here* through God's Spirit and his people. It is far more beautiful and amazing than the kingdom of this world, and it is *breaking in* to this world all the time.

I find hope in looking at the lives of those like Joni Eareckson Tada who offer their suffering for the kingdom's sake. They are honest with their desire for healing, and they are generous to let the body of Christ grieve with them. Their hearts are softened, and they are able to empathize and offer compassion (which means "suffering with" someone) in unique ways. *Love grows there.*

Breathe in: *In my weakness—*
Breathe out: *His power is made perfect.*

Where have you seen the upside-down kingdom at work? Have you seen someone let their weakness show God's power?

Day 29

RETURNING TO HOME BASE

The Lord is near. Do not be anxious about anything, but in every situation, by prayer and petition, with thanksgiving, present your requests to God. And the peace of God, which transcends all understanding, will guard your hearts and your minds in Christ Jesus. (Philippians 4:5–7)

Most of the time, it is incredibly unhelpful for someone to tell us "don't worry" when we're smack dab in the middle of anxiety. Maybe you have wondered, "If I was capable of not worrying, wouldn't I stop whenever I wanted to?"

The only time I feel relief with "don't worry" is when the person saying it has the power to actually speak to my worries. For example, my anxiety shrank when my nephrologist, a doctor who specializes in kidneys, gave me my kidney disease diagnosis and then said, "This is a really good diagnosis. You don't need to worry."

Today's reading starts with power. *The Lord is near.* The One with the ultimate ability to stop, ease, or redeem our anxiety has drawn close to us. And he invites us to draw close to him.

Prayer is one of the main ways we draw close to Jesus. Often we think about prayer as talking to God. But a biblical picture of prayer offers us more. Prayer is connecting with God using not only our thoughts and words but our bodies and emotions as well.

When I'm overwhelmed and without words, I play my prayers on the piano. I lift my emotions to God because he knows my heart better than I know it myself (Psalm 139).

When I'm swarmed by thoughts that I can't seem to quiet, I take my dog for a walk. I orient my delight in her joyful, bouncy trot toward God. He made me to enjoy him through his good creation (Psalm 8:3–4).

When I'm stuck trying to figure out an impossible question, I make a cup of tea and bring my attention to the warmth, the smell, and the lovely flavor. I give God thanks for taste buds and tea leaves, kettles that boil, and comforting mugs.

In the movie *Hook*, Peter Pan's children are kidnapped by Captain Hook and taken to Neverland. Hook begins to brainwash Peter's son, Jack, into becoming a pirate. And bit by bit, Jack forgets where he came from.

In a powerful moment, Jack is up to bat in a baseball game. He has two strikes, and a group of enthusiastic-but-confused pirates begin to chant "Run home, Jack!" instead of "Home run, Jack!" The words *run home* jog Jack's memory. He remembers that his home isn't with the pirates. It's with the ones who love him.

For me, anxiety can look a lot like the amnesia Jack experiences. I'm paralyzed and forgetful, unable to think straight. I'm overwhelmed. But I know if I can get moving, I will make it home. I will run home to Jesus, who offers me peace that passes understanding. He draws near as I'm stuck, and he welcomes me home each time.

In our reading today, we hear about some bases we can run toward when we're stuck in our worries. We're given prayer, petition, and thanksgiving. Prayer is where we address God as I described above. Petition is a more specific asking for what we want and need. And thanksgiving roots us in gratitude and praise.

When God himself invites us not to worry, he does so from a position of power infused with compassion. He is our home base—always ready and near to receive us with his love. As we run to him, we can rest assured he will meet us at every step as he provides for us in our anxiety.

Breathe in: *When I am anxious—*
Breathe out: *The Lord welcomes me home.*

Make a list of three ways you could pray today, three petitions you have for God, and three thanksgivings.

Day 30

ENACTING THE BIGGER STORY

*Let the message of Christ dwell among you richly as
you teach and admonish one another with all wisdom
through psalms, hymns, and songs from the Spirit, singing
to God with gratitude in your hearts. (Colossians 3:16)*

From the beginning of time, all creation has been made to participate in the story of love God is writing. Humans and other creatures and nature alike were all designed to worship our Creator Redeemer. One of the main ways we do this is by *receiving* and *responding* to the One with life-giving, healing power in his voice. It reminds me of the call and response that happened as Aslan sang Narnia into existence in *The Magician's Nephew*.

> In the darkness something was happening at last. A voice had begun to sing. . . . It was so beautiful [Digory] could hardly bear it. . . . Then two wonders happened at the same moment. One was that the voice was suddenly joined by other voices; more voices than you could possibly count. They were in harmony with it, but far higher up the scale. . . . If you had seen and heard it, as Digory did, you would have felt quite certain that it was the first voice, the deep one, which had made them appear and made them sing.[1]

The stars and planets couldn't help but join in the song the First Voice was singing in Lewis's story. It echoes Psalm 19:1, which tells us, "The heavens declare the glory of God, and the sky above proclaims his handiwork" (ESV).

This is a taste of how we've been designed to *receive* and *respond.* We've been given hearts made to come alive to God's beauty, goodness, and love in the world (thereby *receiving*). And we've been given minds, bodies, and spirits made to participate in that Bigger Story by *responding* through praise, wonder, and gratitude to God.

In the verse today, Paul invited us to *receive* by letting the Word of Christ take up residence in us. I imagine him saying, "Let the mystery of God's story enter your ears and dance its way in and through every part of you, seeping into your blood, your breath, and your bones. Let it make its home in you, and make your home in it." This can happen in any number of ways. Paul went on to give us the examples of teaching and guiding one another through psalms, hymns, and songs to God—all with thankfulness in our hearts.

In the act of communal worship (whether at church or in smaller groups), we receive and respond to God's Bigger Story just like the voices in Narnia. We let his truths wash over us, and we declare them as well. Even if our anxiety or depression silences us, we take part as others sing over us the words we cannot.

God invites us to replace our anxious and intrusive worries with the truth of this big and magnificent story he writes us into. Singing and worship don't necessarily stop our anxiety, but they draw our attention to something and someone better. His melody is love and life to the full.

When I am filled with anxiety, worship helps me to enact the bigger, better story of God's kingdom at work. It gathers my attention to the voices singing over me and to the feel of my own as I aim my heart, hands, and head toward King Jesus.

Breathe in: *When my anxiety is loud—*
Breathe out: *May the Bigger Story grow louder.*

What particular song grabs your heart and reminds you of the truths of the Bigger Story?

Day 31

LOOKING TO THE END OF OUR STORY

Look! God's dwelling place is now among the people, and he will dwell with them. They will be his people, and God himself will be with them and be their God. 'He will wipe every tear from their eyes. There will be no more death' or mourning or crying or pain, for the old order of things has passed away. (Revelation 21:3–4)

What if you knew without a doubt that everything was going to be okay?

One of anxiety's go-to lies is that things will never be different. We think to ourselves, "It's always been this way, and it's always going to be this way." Nothing will ever change.

The first time I read through the Harry Potter series, I had a really hard time putting it down. Late into the night, my eyes would droop and my wrists would ache, but I couldn't stop. I wanted to know what happened! The anticipation could even feel like anxiety. Would Hermione and Harry be able to save Hagrid? Would Snape and the Death Eaters take over Hogwarts? Would Voldemort win? No matter what, I kept reading. The momentary discomfort didn't keep me from looking forward to the end.

Whenever I reread the series now, I'm able to enjoy the story in a different way. I have no doubt about how it'll turn out. I still feel the rise and fall of the conflicts. Because I can't remember the details, I still wonder exactly how we're going to get to the ending. But the particularly nerve-wracking moments don't have the same power over me. When worry begins to grip me, I remember that I already know the end of the story.

Because Jesus rose from the dead, we too know the end of our story. Death doesn't win. Satan and his crafty lies don't win. Our anxiety doesn't win either. No, our infinitely creative God is redeeming those things here and now in the pages leading up to the end. Our very worst moments are being worked into something beautiful. God doesn't erase our challenges, struggles, or darkness. Instead, he transforms them. He transforms us.

In our reading today we're told that in the end, God will wipe away every tear. This means he *sees* every tear. He acknowledges our pain. He gives *weight* to our anxiety, our fear, and our losses. And he moves toward us with the gentle care of a good Father.

The end of our story is really a beginning. We will live in the full presence of God, whose light illuminates all things (Revelation 22:5). Here, we live in perfect joy in the vibrant new creation. Our individual stories aren't lost; they are gloriously redeemed into the eternal story. We get to soak in the vivid perfection of colors, music, and mountains. We get to feast on unimaginably delicious food in our glorious resurrection bodies with people from faraway places and times. Here, our earthly anxiety will exist only in the shadow of a memory, for it too will have been redeemed.

In the Christian life, we get to be honest with how hard it is not to be anxious. We get to cry out to the One who empathizes with us, the One who wastes *none* of our pain—the One who came, died, and rose again to secure for us the happiest ending imaginable.

When anxiety whispers the lie "Things will always be this way," we can remember we already know the end of our story: we will have perfect life with Christ forever. We can take courage in looking for how this ending is *already breaking in. Look* for his love displayed in those around you. *Listen* for the sound of his voice in Scripture. *Feel* his air in your lungs. Let the beauty of his creation captivate you as you await its fullness.

Breathe in: *When my anxiety seems endless—*
Breathe out: *I remember the truer, more beautiful end of my story.*

What do you imagine it will be like to be in the full presence of God in the new creation? Spend some time journaling or creating music, art, or poetry in response.

ACKNOWLEDGMENTS

A huge, hearty thank you to each and every teenager who helped bring this book into existence. For all of you who answered my questions (and you *know* I have a fair few), all of you who read bits along the way and provided feedback, and all of you who've let me into your lives over the years. I have learned so much about who Jesus is from you. Abi and Alexa Davis: your help was clutch!

Writing is a little like surfing in a storm; sometimes you have momentum and it's thrilling. Sometimes you're thrown to the ocean floor by a huge wave. Charlotte Getz and Laura Bosco, this book could not have happened without your sage lifeguarding skills. Thank you for your kindness, your encouragement, and your excellent editing midwifery. Chelsea Erickson, my last-lap hero and advocate: you can sniper my darlings any day. Thank you also to Amanda Martin and the team at P&R for cultivating and shaping this project in essential ways!

I am so grateful for the dear friends who surround me: thank you, thank you to North Shore Fellowship, Brewsday, the Weichbrodts, and all my Rooted family. Cameron Cole, your cheerleading from the very beginning has buoyed my soul and changed my life. Meg Day and Kellie Currin, your partnership in ministry and willingness to walk in the trenches with me have brought me closer to Jesus. Danielle Avula, Brittany Crawford, Lo Alcorn, and Anna LaRochelle, your steady, prayerful sisterhood always loops me back to hope. Heather Dirkse, your strength and deep care for me have been nourishing soil. Robby Holt, thank you for *seeing* me and for tirelessly grounding us in the goodness of creation. Christ Episcopal Church, thank you for revealing the beauty of grace to me. Young Life Warrenton, I don't know where I would be without your faithfulness in loving me and showing me Jesus all those years.

To all who've encouraged me by telling me I have something to say—my book club, the MAC class of 2014, Monica Taffinder Tyedmers, Gaye Stone, and Tracy McKay, a million thanks. Jim Coffield and Scott Coupland: your compassion, humility, and wisdom shaped my heart in more ways than I could ever describe. Thank you for fleshing out the love of Jesus over and over. To each client who allowed me to sit with them in their story: thank you so much for the huge honor of letting me be a part of your journey. Your courage and vulnerability have been vital contributing factors to this book.

And to the one who always supports me, always believes in me, and always prays for me—the one who's helped me laugh at the monstrous amount of anxiety caused by writing an anxiety devotional: I love you more than words can say, Mom. Your desire for honesty and your heart for the Lord remain two of my greatest treasures.

Appendix

UNDERSTANDING EMOTIONS

Anxiety is an emotion. Emotions are *energy in motion*, and they tend to show up in our bodies (e.g., neck tightness, clenched jaw, shortness of breath, and a tense stomach). They also tend to grow thoughts ("What if they don't like me?" "What if I do something stupid?" "What if I fail?" "I'm an awkward person").

Sometimes anxiety develops because we haven't *identified* and *felt* our way through other emotions in the presence of someone who loves us.

In Genesis, God invited Adam to name the animals he had created (2:19), and then he told Adam to take care of them (1:28). When we take time to label our emotions, it allows us to then steward them better.

A feelings wheel is a great place to learn about what the emotions actually are. We often use phrases like "I feel like he's mad at me" or "It feels like something is wrong" to describe our feelings. But these are not emotions. They are interpretations of our emotions. Those statements often have actual emotions fueling them, so we can check in with our options for actual emotions on the feelings wheel. For example, you may be feeling worried and upset underneath the "I feel like he's mad at me" statement. Or you may be feeling guilty, anxious, and sad underneath the "It feels like something is wrong" statement.

Once we identify and name our emotions, we can do the hard (and super important) work of sharing them with safe, trusted people around us and with the Lord. We are made to be *known* and *loved* in our emotions and to bear them with one another.

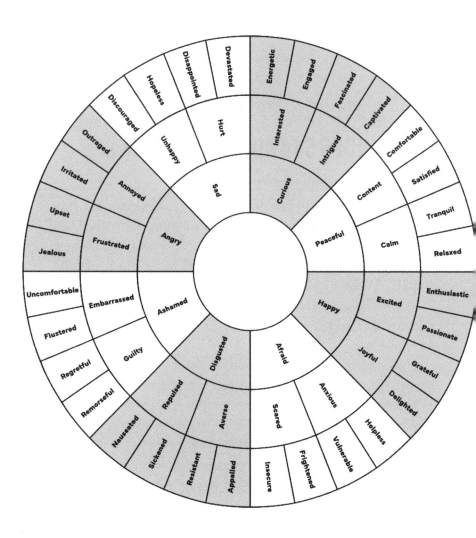

Labeling our emotions can also help us to see what thoughts and stories they've been growing.

Sometimes our emotions write false stories about who we are. Did feeling shy in class grow the story "I am an awkward person"? Did feeling embarrassed that you didn't make the basketball team grow the lie "I am worthless"?

Sometimes they write false stories about others. Take social media, for example. As we scroll through the images, our loneliness, jealousy, and shame may grow the story "Their lives are all perfect. They have it so much better than me."

It is helpful to separate out our thoughts and feelings so that we can identify who or what we're listening to. Emotions need to be named, felt, and stewarded. We want to listen to and honor them so that they aren't ruling over us without us realizing it. They shift and change, whereas Jesus Christ is the same yesterday, today, and forever (Hebrews 13:8).

The best Ruler for our thoughts, emotions, and behaviors is King Jesus, the one who is *himself* Truth. By naming our emotions and the stories they grow, we can then place them under the kingship of the God who loves us and knows us to our core. As the psalmists in the Bible do, we can bring God all that we're feeling—whether we are angry, sad, joyful, or anxious. He meets us right as we are, and he walks compassionately with us. He himself experienced a great deal of emotions, having walked the earth as a human. He is the ultimate empathizer.

He is also the Way, the Truth, and the Life (John 14:6). This means that we can check all the stories our hearts and minds tell us with his truth to see what is accurate. We spend time in his Word, prayer, and fellowship with other believers to do just that.

NOTES

DAY 3: ORDER FROM CHAOS

1. William David Reyburn and Euan McGregor Fry, *A Handbook on Genesis* (Philadelphia: American Bible Society, 1997), 30.

DAY 22: GOD HOLDS US TOGETHER

1. Kuyper's inaugural address at the dedication of the Free University, quoted in *Abraham Kuyper: A Centennial Reader*, ed. James D. Bratt (Grand Rapids: Eerdmans, 1998), 488.

DAY 27: GIVING OUR ALLEGIANCE TO KING JESUS

1. Timothy Keller and Kathy Keller, *The Meaning of Marriage: Facing the Complexities of Commitment with the Wisdom of God* (New York: Penguin Books, 2011), 68.

DAY 30: ENACTING THE BIGGER STORY

1. C. S. Lewis, *The Magician's Nephew* (New York: HarperCollins, 1955), 115–16.

 rooted

Rooted Ministry's mission is to equip and empower churches and parents to faithfully disciple students toward life-long faith in Jesus Christ. Our vision is to transform youth and family ministry so that every student receives grace-filled, gospel-centered and Bible-saturated discipleship in the church and at home.

Rooted was born in response to the crisis in the spiritual lives of young people. What started with a small conference has grown into a movement to see gospel-centered youth ministry become the normative experience of teenagers throughout the church. Rooted promotes gospel-centered youth ministry through conferences, regional groups, Rooted Reservoir (our video training and curriculum), blog, podcasts, and books. Rooted's 2021 release, *The Jesus I Wish I Knew in High School*, features stories from thirty authors about bullying, eating disorders, addiction, racism, family conflict, and the intense pressure to achieve, demonstrating how knowing Jesus brings rest and healing.

Rooted embraces a simple approach to youth ministry based on our understanding of Scripture and validated by research on effective models for cultivating sustainable faith in young people. We emphasize five pillars of youth ministry which include gospel centrality, theological depth through biblical teaching, relational discipleship, partnership with parents, and integration with the whole church body.

Rooted uses this framework to promote faithful discipleship of young people through the adults who love them. Imagine the impact on teenagers' lives if each week they are taught God's Word, prayed for, and mentored to understand God's grace for them through Christ. Rooted is reaching thousands of students by equipping their leaders for this type of meaningful ministry.

To learn more about Rooted, visit www.rootedministry.com.